Satan attacks a pastor in various ways. S
and scandalous sins. However, sometim
distracts us from what is most important
an excuse to neglect another duty. He su
us act as if we have no needs or limitatio..... ....
dangers, and is eminently helpful to preserve a pastor for long-term service
to the glory of God. I heartily recommend it for men aspiring to ministry,
for men in ministry, and for all those who love them.

—Joel R. Beeke, President, Puritan Reformed Theological Seminary,
Grand Rapids, Michigan

I have never met Al Martin in the flesh. Yet, if I were to name ten men whose
lives and ministries have been anchors for me in the midst of the tumultuous
spiritual storms of pastoral ministry in Africa, his name would certainly
feature prominently on that list. Partly, this is because at a formative stage
in my ministry I came across his messages on "Ministerial Backsliding and
Burnout". So, I am delighted to know that these messages are being given
a fresh lease of life through this book and being made available to a new
generation of ministers. For sure, I owe an incalculable debt to the truths
contained in these pages.

—Conrad Mbewe, Pastor of Kabwata Baptist Church, Lusaka, Zambia

Pastor Martin has been lifting me up from day one of my ministry when
the first thing I did was start listening to his lectures on pastoral ministry.
Since then, God has repeatedly and mightily used that practical counsel
in my life to prevent backsliding and credibility washout. The one time
in my life I did come close to burnout was because I had briefly and
stupidly ignored his tried and tested practical advice, something I quickly
rectified. I'm so thankful that Pastor Martin's years of pastoral experience
and wisdom are now being made available to the church in this wonderful
book. I believe it will save many ministries and spare many families and
churches the grief of burned-out, knocked-out, and washed-out pastors.

—David Murray, Professor of Old Testament and Practical Theology,
Puritan Reformed Theological Seminary, Grand Rapids, Michigan

This is an honest, incisive, and realistic treatment of the subject of ministerial
burnout. There is a most helpful mixture here of spiritual insight and
commonsense, and the result should be of benefit to all pastors in Christ's flock,
and ultimately to the flock itself. Ministerial burnout has reached epidemic
proportions in many parts of the world, and this work could be much used to
alleviate that situation. The eight specific warnings are all well-handled from
Scripture, history, and pastoral experience. May it do much good!

—Peter Barnes, Author, lecturer, Revesby Presbyterian Church, Revesby,
New South Wales, Australia

We are thankful to have in these pages the wisdom and experience of a preacher to whom so many of us are indebted.

—Iain Murray, Co-founder of Banner of Truth, Edinburgh, Scotland

How thrilling was Albert Martin's arrival on the scene in England in the late 60s. He seemed to have taken all that was the very best of evangelical preaching from the Puritans, and the preachers of the Evangelical Awakening, from M'Cheyne in Scotland and from Princeton in New Jersey, from Ryle and Spurgeon, from reading of John Murray's book *Redemption: Accomplished and Applied*, and he mined all this rich seam of experiential Calvinism and he brought out jewels. He preached to the mind, affections and consciences of his hearers and impacted them so that in the succeeding years as he returned to our conferences the numbers increased. God's blessing was on him and on us. What we experienced in England was also replicated in the USA. Now in retirement from the pastorate this substantial work has appeared. It is on a theme familiar enough to the Puritans, on ministerial credibility and backsliding. How discerning and searching our fathers were in analysing the marks of such declension and the means of ministerial revival. May this be the first of a number of books to come from Albert Martin to the good of the whole church, especially its servants the preachers.

—Geoff Thomas, Pastor, Alfred Place Baptist Church, Aberystwyth, Wales

Quite a few books are being written today to benefit pastors in their ministries. Not many however seem to help practically in or from times of personal failure. Such is the goal of Al Martin's *You Lift Me Up: Overcoming ministry challenges.*

The author brings to this volume a lifetime of Christian ministry, studious preparation and experience in teaching pastors. He brings warnings and solutions to such problems as when men neglect their devotional lives or family responsibilities, wander from a good conscience or from real fellowship with their people. Balanced help is offered against opposing dangers: being over-devoted to perceived pastoral needs or focusing only on sermon preparation. Ministers are not to work at hiding their real humanity from those among whom the Lord has placed them, nor, on the other hand, to allow over-eating and lack of exercise to demonstrate their undisciplined behaviour!

Al Martin has two main audiences here, from whom few pastors are excluded: men who need to correct themselves and be restored – and those who may be helped to avoid such mistakes. May this book transform and help to sustain many of us.

—Ted Donnelly, Principal, Reformed Theological College, Belfast, Northern Ireland

You Lift Me Up

Overcoming ministry challenges

Albert N. Martin

ⲘENTOR

Unless otherwise indicated Scripture quotations are taken from *The Holy Bible, English Standard Version*, copyright © 2001 by Crossway Bibles, a division of Good News Publishers. Used by permission. All rights reserved. ESV. Text Edition: 2007

Scripture quotations marked KJV are taken from the *King James Version*. All rights reserved.

Albert Martin served as pastor of Trinity Baptist Church in Montville, New Jersey, for more than forty years, and he taught Pastoral Theology in the Trinity Ministerial Academy for twenty years. Esteemed by leading theologians and pastors, his preaching is the subject of a book, *My Heart for Thy Cause* (978-1-85792-716-0).

Copyright © Albert N. Martin 2013

paperback ISBN 978-1-78191-227-0
epub ISBN 978-1-78191-278-2
Mobi ISBN 978-1-78191-279-9

10 9 8 7 6 5 4 3 2 1

Published in 2013
by
Christian Focus Publications Ltd,
Geanies House, Fearn,
Ross-shire, IV20 1TW, Scotland.
www.christianfocus.com

Cover design
by
Daniel van Straaten

Printed by
Bell and Bain, Glasgow

CONTENTS

To D. Scott Meadows:

   —True friend
   — Beloved brother in Christ
   — Respected Pastor

Without whose labors this book would not be in your hands

Introduction

A Brief Account of This Material's Present Form

At the 1990 pastors' conference of Trinity Baptist Church in Montville, New Jersey, I was privileged to speak at six plenary sessions. My chosen theme was 'Warnings Against Ministerial Backsliding and Burnout'. During the conference many of the men testified to the unusual benefit which they received from those messages.

Since then others have indicated to me that the recordings of those messages have continued to be useful. Some of those encouragements came in the form of urgings to put the matter into print. Those urgings, along with my growing personal conviction that there is a great need for these truths, led to this book. Some of the very men who attended that 1990 conference are now shameful and tragic monuments of the wreckage which often follows ministerial backsliding and burnout.

In converting the original lectures into printed form, I have sought to maintain the ethos of direct address, a crucial element in effective preaching. While working on the manuscript I have tried to picture a group of godly pastors sitting before me, eager to recognize in themselves the signs of ministerial backsliding or burnout, and equally eager to apply the biblical and practical remedies to these twin conditions.

While reworking the material I realized that the final warning moves into a third area of concern. I have called this concern 'credibility washout.' When the reader comes to the last two chapters containing the eighth warning, the intended sense of the phrase 'credibility washout' will become clear.

These lectures were delivered under the title *Ministerial Backsliding, Burnout – Symptoms, Causes, And Cures.* In preparing the original manuscript from the transcribed lectures, I used that title as the framework for this book. My editors at Christian Focus and I found that the present title, *You Lift Me Up*, more concisely embodies the contents and encourages the pastor in ministry. Given that it would have been quite difficult to go back and rework the material to make it more consistent with the new title or to omit from the text all references to the old title, I hope that this explanation will assist the reader in answering any questions growing out of any perceived disparity between this book's title and its contents.

Prayers offered before and after the lectures are reproduced with minor editorial changes. I trust they will in some measure echo the disposition with which the reader approaches the material and confirm the response of each reader to the things contained in the lectures. Some of the original prayers were not recorded and are therefore omitted.

For some these pages, with God's blessing, will prove corrective and restorative. For others they may prove preventive. In either case I send them forth with the prayer that the Great Shepherd of the sheep will use them to help many of His under-shepherds.

Albert N. Martin
Jenison, Michigan 2012

ONE

What Is Ministerial Backsliding and Burnout?

My initial task will be to define the terms of our title, 'ministerial backsliding and burnout'.

First, what do I mean by the words 'ministerial backsliding'? In using these words I am referring to several aspects of spiritual experience. First of all, I am referring to that erosion of spiritual reality, spiritual vigor and spiritual growth which can overtake a man of God, often imperceptibly, even in the midst of the most active and externally-faithful ministerial labors. I am alluding to a declension which is manifested, not immediately in the pulpit, but rather in the prayer closet. It is a declension which may not be discerned at all in the substance of a man's teaching and preaching, but in the degree to which the fire and passion of the truths he conveys to others have lost much of their felt impression upon his own heart. In the deep chambers of his heart, in the quiet moments of honest self-examination, the haunting awareness of his condition stabs his conscience. His ministerial backsliding becomes a gnawing irritation of the soul, constantly reminding the man that all is not now as it once was between himself and his God.

Ministerial backsliding also describes that condition which prevails when a man of God has declined in his grace-motivated, Spirit-enabled, scrupulous obedience to the revealed will of God. Jesus said, 'Whoever has my commandments and keeps them, he it is who loves me. And he who loves me will be loved by my Father, and I will love him and manifest myself to him' (John 14:21). When love burns toward the Savior a sincere passion to render obedience to all of His precepts is our desire, our delight and our holy obsession. When a man begins to pick and choose which commands he will obey so that the honest pursuit of what the old writers called 'universal obedience' is no longer his holy obsession, he has entered a backslidden state. A spiritually-healthy man can say with the psalmist, 'Therefore I consider all your precepts to be right; I hate every false way' (Ps. 119:128). He can also pray from the heart these words of the psalmist: 'Oh that my ways may be steadfast in keeping your statutes! Then I shall not be put to shame, having my eyes fixed on all your commandments' (Ps. 119:5-6).

This backsliding may eventually come to expression in the outcropping of specific forms of carnality. Laziness, self-indulgence, peevishness and a host of other sins which, while not quite scandalous, begin to manifest themselves and deeply affect a man's usefulness as he lives and labors among his family and his flock. By ministerial backsliding I mean a condition in which we reflect the opposite of that which the apostle Paul enjoined upon his spiritual son Timothy in 1 Timothy 4:15: 'Practice these things, immerse yourself in them, *so that all may see your progress.*'

Second, what about the phrase 'ministerial burnout'? You may say, 'I have read my Bible through 40 times and have never encountered the term "ministerial burnout".' Since strictly speaking it is not a biblical term, I ought to supply a precise definition of my intended meaning. I am referring to a gradual erosion of one's mental, emotional, psychological, and physical resiliency and buoyancy which begins to hang like an ominous dark cloud over the entirety of one's life and ministry. Like ministerial backsliding, this condition can overtake us in the context of a very active and faithful ministry. I am not referring to the inevitable declension in physical and mental strength which may be part of the normal aging process – that which the apostle Paul designated as the 'wasting away' of our outer nature (2 Cor. 4:16).

Rather, ministerial burnout has overtaken us when our mental activities are not occasionally dull and sluggish, but chronically and overwhelmingly dull and sluggish. We are afflicted with this condition when serious and concentrated study becomes a crushing and galling burden. When the appointed hour comes to engage in the labor of serious exegetical spadework, instead of coming to that task with mental alacrity and spiritual excitement, we find ourselves under necessity to whip ourselves to the desk. We also find that we must whip ourselves while engaged in the task itself. When we leave our desks, we are further whipped by a condemning conscience. Even though we have the privilege of rooting around in the Word of God – and the benefit of being paid for our labors – we feel that we are miserable wretches because we have come to consider this privileged labor a wearisome burden.

Further, by ministerial burnout I am referring to that mental condition in which the particularly inventive and creative elements of sermon preparation such as organization, illustration, application, and imagery, seem to elude our powers. When we attempt to fix our minds on a mass of exegetical and homiletical material that desperately needs sorting and putting into acceptable rhetorical categories, we are powerless to discern one brick of thought from another, to decide the right pile for any given brick, and then how to build all those raw materials into a well-constructed sermon. At times we may even come perilously close to taking all the results of our labors, now embedded in our study notes, and sweep them off our desks and onto the floor saying to ourselves that there must be a more suitable way to serve God and to make an honest living! My dear reader, I have been in that condition more than once.

Furthermore, in identifying the nature of ministerial burnout, I am referring to that condition in which we lose most of our ability to feel deeply concerning the great realities in which we constantly traffic. The emotions which ought naturally to accompany us in the secret place and in our public and private ministries to the people of God seem almost neutered.

At another level ministerial burnout refers to our condition when physical energy and resiliency have left us, and so that even one additional or unusual demand may leave us in a heap for days. Or, from a legitimate sense of self-preservation, we may avoid opportunities to do good because we dread the subsequent weariness and weakness that will surely come on the heels of taking on that additional burden. Can you as a pastor and a preacher relate to anything I have said in describing ministerial backsliding and burnout?

Let me add a word of qualification. By these definitions and descriptions I am not in any way implying that there are not divinely-appointed seasons in our lives and ministries in which there will be a different range of spiritual, emotional, intellectual and even physical vigor as part of the ebb and flow of normal Christian experience. There are indeed sovereignly-imposed periods of spiritual desertion and sovereignly-imposed seasons of spiritual discipline that may find expression in physical and mental weakness or in emotional dullness (see Isa. 50:10-11; Ps.56-57; 88). However, what I am saying is that as an ordinary rule the servants of God ought not to be carrying on their ministries in a prevailing state of ministerial backsliding or ministerial burnout as I have described them. The norm of our lives and ministries should be a fulfillment of that which is beautifully expressed in Psalm 92:12-15 where God promises, 'The righteous flourish like the palm tree and grow like a cedar in Lebanon. They are planted in the house of the LORD; they flourish in the courts of our God. They still bear fruit in old age; they are ever full of sap and green, to declare that the LORD is upright; he is my rock, and there is no unrighteousness in him.'

With advancing years many men become brittle and sapless. Rather than becoming the epitome of ripened godliness, spiritual vigor and ministerial energy, they become like dried trees – half dead, with autumn leaves barely hanging upon them and with very little fruitfulness. With promises like Psalm 92 to encourage us, why should we accept ministerial backsliding or burnout as a tolerable norm?

Now that I have defined and described what I mean by the terms ministerial backsliding and burnout, it is my purpose to set before you eight specific warnings relative to these two conditions. The first three focus primarily upon ministerial backsliding. The fourth is a transition concern that applies to both conditions. The last four focus primarily upon ministerial burnout. The final warning also moves into the area that I have chosen to call 'credibility washout'. I will define that term when it is first used in connection with the final warning. While there is some overlapping and interpenetration of these things, each of the warnings is distinct enough to warrant a separate treatment.

WARNINGS

AGAINST

MINISTERIAL BACKSLIDING

Two

Beware of Distractions from Devotion

Warning number one is this: if you would avoid ministerial backsliding, *beware of allowing the demands of your official ministerial duties to erode the disciplines of the devotional nurture of your own soul.*

I would be greatly surprised if each of my readers did not at one time or another hear the old dictum that 'the life of the minister is the life of his ministry'. Those words are simply one man's way of attempting to express what the Holy Spirit has said to us in two of the most pivotal passages in Scripture with reference to our primary ministerial duties.

The first of these is Acts 20:28. Paul is charging the Ephesian elders (that is, pastors) with their solemn responsibilities now that he is about to leave them. Henceforth, the care of the church will be entirely upon their shoulders under the Lordship of Christ. Paul's words to these elders are: 'Pay careful attention (that is, pay constant and close attention) to yourselves and to all the flock, in which the Holy Spirit has made you overseers'. As these elders no doubt reflected upon and discussed together Paul's exhortation to them, I wonder what their thinking and the substance of their conversation might have been. Would they not have been surprised to hear Paul insisting their fundamental and primary responsibility was taking heed to themselves? In those words Paul was saying to them in effect, 'You men are God's chosen instruments through whom Christ will carry on the work of caring for His flock at Ephesus. As is the instrument, so will be the work. Therefore, you must above all else take heed to yourselves. Only then will you be fit to take care of the flock in which the Holy Spirit has made you overseers.' God has never rescinded that divine order of priority concerning the fundamental responsibilities of pastors.

The second passage is 1 Timothy 4:16. After Paul laid upon Timothy a vast spectrum of ministerial duties in conjunction with ordering and superintending behavior in the house of God at Ephesus (1 Tim. 3:15-16), he then turns his attention to Timothy himself (4:6 ff.). His exhortations to Timothy culminate in verse 16 where he says to him, 'Keep a close watch (again, pay constant, close and careful attention) on yourself and on the teaching. Persist in this.' Persist in what? Obviously, the things just mentioned, namely the constant care and nurture of himself and of his teaching. Then Paul buttresses his exhortation by reminding Timothy of the blessed results that will come from his obedience to the clear directions concerning his responsibility to engage in a constant and careful watch over himself and over his teaching. He promises Timothy that in the course of his compliance with these directives he will both save himself and those that hear him. Paul clearly says to his spiritual son and ministerial colleague that his own personal salvation is to be his first and fundamental responsibility. Only as he fulfills that responsibility can he be assured that he will be an instrument in the hands of God to secure the salvation of his hearers.

In spite of these two passages with their unmistakably clear directives, it is a tragic reality that all too often we allow our conscientious pursuit of our ministerial duties to the flock to become the occasion of neglecting the nurture of our own souls. Let me describe the descent into a state of ministerial backsliding.

I doubt it is possible to find one preacher in a thousand who was found on any given Monday morning enjoying a rich, fruitful devotional nurture of his own soul as his primary ministerial exercise who then, by Tuesday morning, had degenerated into a backslidden state – a state in which the devotional reading of the Word of God, self-examination, prayer for increased communion with and conformity to Christ had been all but abandoned. No! It is a much more subtle process of erosion. A little neglect here and a little neglect there. The process goes on until, alas, sometimes it takes a grievous fall to bring a man back to the place where he says to himself, 'How did I get to the position where I could fall into this horrible sin?' He looks back and then discovers that there had been a subtle, almost imperceptible, process of erosion in the disciplines connected with the nurture of his own soul. You see, my brethren, the means ordained of God for the nurture and ongoing health of the inner life of a pastor are not one bit different than they are for any child of God, regardless of his or her calling.

While writing this book I have been rereading John Owen's treatise, 'The Grace and Duty of Being Spiritually Minded'. He addresses this very issue when he writes:

> Take heed of decays! Whatever ground the Gospel loseth in our minds, sin possesseth it for itself and its own ends. Let none say it is otherwise with them. Men grow cold and negligent in the duties of Gospel worship, public and private; which is to reject Gospel light. Let them say and pretend

what they please, that in other things, in their minds and conversations, it is well with them: indeed it is not so. Sin will, sin doth, one way or other, make an increase in them proportionate unto these decays, and will sooner or later discover itself so to do; and themselves, if they are not utterly hardened, may greatly discover it, inwardly in their peace, or outwardly in their lives.[1]

THE BIBLE

Among the means ordained by God for the nurture of the inner life, none is more vital than assimilating the Word of God in a prayerful and reflective frame of mind and heart. This assimilation should always involve honest self-examination, but of the kind expressed by David in his prayer at the end of Psalm 139:23-24, 'Search me, O God, and know my heart! Try me and know my thoughts! And see if there be any grievous way in me, and lead me in the way everlasting!' This assimilation must be structured and regular. In it we come to the Word of God as disciples to be taught by our Lord, and not as ministers to receive material for teaching others. In it we come to sit at our Savior's feet – not primarily to learn what we should speak in His name to others, but to know what He would speak in His own name and Person to our own hearts. This is what I mean by the devotional assimilation of the Scriptures.

Jeremiah expressed it beautifully when he wrote, 'Your words were found, and I ate them, and your words became to me a joy and the delight of my heart, for I am called by your name, O LORD, God of hosts' (Jer. 15:16). Or, in the language of the first Psalm, the blessed and fruitful man is the one who meditates on the law of God day and night. The law of God (that is, the whole of inscripturated revelation) is his own internal delight, the meat upon which he feeds his own soul, and that drink by which he refreshes his own inner life.

Hear the challenging words of Thomas Murphy:

---

1   John Owen *The Works of John Owen*, VII, (W.H; Goold, Ed. Edinburgh: T&T Clark), p. 354.

To every pastor, then, would we say, Study the Bible with constant and close self-application. Make its chapters and verses familiar, not merely by the effort to gain an intellectual understanding of them, but by the blessed comfort you have found from them in your own souls. Adopt some rule of *systematic devotional reading*, and let it not be intermitted for any trivial consideration. Let your study of the word be profound, so as to get down to its very marrow and sweetness. Let your meditations be constant, so that all the day long you may have some Scripture before the mind. Let it be with you as his biographer says of McCheyne, that 'he fed on the word, not in order to prepare himself for his people, but for personal edification. To do so was a fundamental rule with him.' And let all this devotional study of the word be mingled with prayer, that the same Spirit who inspired it would give it life and power in its effects upon your own soul.[2]

Our blessed Lord was the great pattern of One who assimilated the words of His heavenly Father in this regular and structured way. It is none other than the Servant of the Lord (a title of Jesus) who says in Isaiah 50:4, 'The Lord GOD has given me the tongue of those who are taught, that I may know how to sustain with a word him who is weary. Morning by morning he awakens; he awakens my ear to hear as those who are taught.' According to this passage our Lord's ability to speak as He spoke to the refreshment, instruction and conviction of others had its taproot in the fact that His own ear was wakened morning by morning to hear the voice of His heavenly Father. Remember the words of John, 'whoever says he abides in him ought to walk in the same way in which he walked' (1 John 2:6).

---

2   Thomas Murphy, D.D., *Pastoral Theology* (Philadelphia, Pennsylvania: Presbyterian Board of Publication and Sabbath School Work, 1887), pp. 78-79. Dr. Murphy served for more than 25 years in the Frankford Presbyterian Church in Philadelphia. During his seminary training in Princeton he was privileged to sit under the lectures of Dr. Archibald Alexander. He freely acknowledges his great indebtedness to the formative influence of that great man of God upon the perspectives embodied in this book.

Prayer

And then, of course, another vital discipline of the inner life is the maintenance of the habit and spirit of secret prayer. Jesus said that men 'ought always to pray and not lose heart' (Luke 18:1). The apostle Paul concluded his description of the Christian's armor with the exhortation that the people of God are to be found 'praying at all times in the Spirit, with all prayer and supplication. To that end keep alert with all perseverance, making supplication for all the saints' (Eph. 6:18). We must maintain both the habit and the spirit of secret prayer. As the old writers said, 'We must be determined to pray until we have prayed.' We must not be content that we have merely spent a fixed time in an activity that we call prayer. Rather, we should be restless and discontent if in those times of prayer a pattern emerges in which we have had no conscious engagement of God Himself, no conscious enlargement of desire after God, no conscious communion with Christ and no conscious breaking up of the fallow ground of our hearts. If we do not maintain the habit and spirit of secret prayer it will only be a matter of time before a chronic chill of backsliding will set in upon our souls.

Spiritual reading

Then I believe there is a peculiar responsibility and opportunity laid upon those of us set apart from the ordinary means of employment in order to 'labor in the word and in doctrine'. Not only should we engage in the two disciplines already addressed – disciplines which the Word of God makes plain are the duties and privileges of all believers – but I would urge you to consider a further discipline calculated to nurture the inner man. Though I have no biblical warrant to bind anyone's conscience to this activity, I believe it is reasonable as well as profitable to engage in it.

Furthermore, there is a rich and historical precedent for this particular discipline: exposing our minds and hearts on a regular basis to those men and their writings who are masters of the believer's inner life. Consider the words of J. W. Alexander writing to men who aspire to be and already are ministers of the Gospel:

> I hope you will let no kind of reading keep you from looking daily, if only for five minutes, into a class of writers who are not attractive in regard to letters, but who unite great talents, great Bible knowledge, and great unction. At the head of these stands Owen. My father used to say that one should read Owen's *Spiritual Mindedness* once a year.[3]

God's servants have often testified to the blessing that has come to them when they have set themselves down in the presence of God and taken up one of these masters of the inner life with a view to the nurture of their own walk with God. With one of these old masters in their hands they have prayed, 'Oh Lord, this man whose writings I take into my hands is a unique gift of the risen Christ to His church. Use his words to instruct me, to search me, to stir me, to convict me, and above all, to show me my Savior.' How often God has used these men and their writings to minister deeply and profoundly to my own heart! I am not at all suggesting there are no modern 'masters of the inner life' whose writings can be of great profit to us. However, time has proven the great worth of these older works; we rob ourselves of immense blessing if we do not tap in to that rich legacy. However, even though some of us may have known rich blessing in the past through our interaction with such writers, we have by degrees allowed the pressure of our official ministerial duties to crowd out such reading. Our subsequent incipient backsliding is an eloquent witness to our folly. Perhaps

---

3   *Thoughts on Preaching*, p. 93. To these suggestions of Alexander, I would add Owen's *Works*, Volumes 1, 3, 6, and 7. Also, John Flavel's *Works*, Volume 1, 'The Fountain of Life', and Volume 5, 'A Saint Indeed'. Although I have not read any of these once a year, even as I compose these pages I am reading for the seventh time Volume 7 of Owen on *Spiritual Mindedness*. Each time is like the first time. I constantly marvel at how much profound truth I can so quickly forget. It is this tragic reality that drives me back again and again to this kind of reading.

it is time to call to mind the words of the risen Christ to the church at Ephesus, 'Remember therefore from where you have fallen; repent, and do the works you did at first' (Rev. 2:5).

Seasons of protracted waiting upon God

In our effort to resist or to recover from ministerial backsliding there is one final discipline I would commend. I refer to seasons of protracted waiting upon God, seasons of intense self-examination, seasons, if necessary, of fasting joined to prayer. Even though there may be consistency in the ordinary disciplines aimed at keeping our souls in a healthy state, so powerful are the actions of indwelling sin, so subtle are the seductions of the world, and so insidious are the machinations of the Devil, we can be afflicted with an almost imperceptible form of ministerial backsliding if we do not periodically give ourselves to seasons of protracted waiting upon God.

We can become like a sailing vessel that has no leaks in its hull but has picked up a barnacle here and a barnacle there, more barnacles here and yet more barnacles there, until the whole hull is infested with barnacles. Although the sails are hoisted and properly trimmed the mariner somehow senses that the ship is not plowing through the water at its ordinary speed. He checks the automatic bilge pumps, and because they are not active, he knows that the ship is not drawing any water, and the sails have no rips. What does he need to do? He knows he must put his ship into dry dock as soon as possible to expose the hull and scrape off the barnacles. We need times in a spiritual 'dry dock' to scrape from our souls the spiritual barnacles impeding our walk with God. The prophet Jeremiah said, 'Let us test and examine our ways' (Lam. 3:40). If we are not concerned enough about this issue of maintaining spiritual vigor occasionally to block out everything from our schedules other than intense and serious dealings with God, sooner or later it is most likely that we will begin to suffer one or more of the manifestations of ministerial backsliding.

APPLICATION

So, my fellow servant of God, I issue this first warning: beware of allowing the demands of your official ministerial duties to erode the disciplines of the devotional nurture of your own soul. The human heart is so deceitful. We are quite capable of willingly and quickly deceiving ourselves. If we do not keep some kind of a record of what we have read in the Word of God, and how long it has taken us to get from Genesis to Revelation, we will continually fool ourselves. Do not allow yourself the luxury of vague notions as to whether or not you are reading through the whole compass of the Word of God for the nurture of your own soul at least once every year or two. Whatever your Bible reading schedule may be, you must be certain that you are soaking your soul in 'every word that comes from the mouth of God'.

Furthermore, we must not kid ourselves that we are maintaining the habit and spirit of secret prayer without keeping some account of ourselves. You might be shocked if after reading these pages you said to yourself, 'I purpose to spend half an hour in prayer for the needs of my own soul. I am going to give myself to earnest prayer that God would search me and try me to the end that Christ will become more precious to me, that sin will become more odious, and that my pursuit of universal holiness will be intensified.' You may find that the spiritual muscles essential for a half-hour of concentrated prayer have so atrophied that you find yourself prayed out after 17 minutes! It may shock you to recognize this very tangible evidence of incipient backsliding. God can use the clock to bring you into touch with spiritual reality!

I am fully aware that this suggestion is vulnerable to abuse. There is in all of us the spirit of the Pharisee that would measure devotion to God by time, place and activities. However, with respect to these counsels, that is not my practical danger, and I doubt it is yours either. My practical danger is not that of praying for half an hour and then thinking I have earned some

27

brownie points with God. Rather, it is getting so pressured by the work of the ministry that I lose the spiritual vigor that would keep me on my knees for half an hour, clock or no clock. Many times we drive ourselves to self-deception by conjuring up ghosts from the supposed abuse of the very activity which, if embraced and implemented, would precipitate the blessing of God, be the means of our spiritual quickening or our preservation from backsliding. So I beg you, my brother, if you would avoid ministerial backsliding, then heed this first warning. Do not allow the demands of ministerial duties to erode the disciplines required for the nurture of your own soul. This is indeed your primary ministerial responsibility.

Closing Prayer

Our Father, as we bow in Your holy presence, we confess with shame how often we have willfully deceived ourselves. How often we have experienced the eroding effect of neglecting these disciplines through which You have ordained to nurture the inner life of Your servants. We confess with shame that we have dishonored You by this neglect. We have injected a chill and barrenness into our ministries, a lack of discernment into our pastoral dealings, and have produced the other horrible fruits that grow from such neglect. We stand ashamed before the sight of them. Wash us afresh in the blood of Your Son. Put into our hearts the resolutions and the strength to do whatever must be done so that whatever else we are, we may be men who know You in the secret place. Seal these exhortations to our hearts, we plead in Jesus' name. Amen.

THREE

Beware of Neglecting Generic Christian Duties

We come now to consider the second warning for the avoidance of ministerial backsliding, and it is this: *beware of thinking that the performance of specific ministerial duties justifies or excuses the non-performance of generic Christian duties, especially with regard to one's family.*

When I speak of 'specific ministerial duties', I am referring first of all to those spiritual activities connected with fulfilling the responsibilities addressed in the previous chapter, starting with the consistent engagement in the disciplines essential for paying careful attention to ourselves (1 Tim. 4:16; Acts 20:28). Then there are the duties which grow out of our responsibility to 'care for the church of God'. Paramount among them is the privilege of consistently preparing and delivering in the power of the Holy Spirit sermons that are exegetically accurate, theologically balanced, Bible-saturated, Christ-suffused, well-structured, helpfully illustrated and conscience-gripping – sermons that are calculated to nourish the people of God and to summon the unconverted to repentance and faith (2 Tim. 4:2; Acts 20:21).

Next in importance is our responsibility to give close, loving, discerning, personal and biblically-framed instruction, exhortation and admonition to the individual sheep committed to our pastoral charge (Col. 1:28; 1 Thess. 2:11-12; 5:12-13). After this there are those specific administrative pastoral responsibilities which are part of the general directive to 'care for God's church' (1 Tim. 3:5). These things distill the 'specific ministerial duties' identified in Scripture.

What, then, are your 'generic Christian duties'? These are those duties addressed to you simply as a Christian man in your various God-ordained relationships and responsibilities. For example, when the Scriptures say, 'husbands, be this', or 'do that', and you happen to have a wife, then everything addressed to husbands applies directly to you. With respect to those duties and privileges towards your wife there is to be no negation, suspension or dilution of your obedience to them simply because you have to fulfill a host of demanding specific ministerial responsibilities. For example, when Peter counsels the elders in the churches of Asia Minor to 'shepherd the flock of God' (1 Pet. 5.2), he is not exempting these men from his previous exhortation, 'Likewise, husbands, live with your wives in an understanding way, showing honor to the woman as the weaker vessel' (1 Pet. 3:7).

In a similar way, everything said to fathers as fathers applies to you if you are a father. Everything required of Christians in their relationship to civil authorities is spoken directly to you. Everything included in the directives of the fifth commandment applies to you. Remember how Jesus looked upon religious leaders who used the performance of religious duties to rationalize their neglect of the fifth commandment.

He called them hypocrites and characterized their religious activities as worship 'in vain' (Matt. 15:1-9). All the duties of church members are also yours. Even the command to 'obey your leaders and submit to them' (Heb. 13:17) is for you if you have fellow elders. Regardless of your higher profile in public ministry, you still are responsible to fulfill this particular generic duty of the ordinary Christian.

Having defined the significant words contained in this warning, let us consider that the heart of it is this: beware of ever thinking and then acting as if you had a special dispensation from God to be apathetic about or careless in the performance of any generic Christian duty, simply because you are responsible for manifold specific ministerial duties.

Allow me to develop this perspective a bit further. The character requirements for occupying the pastoral office clearly indicate that, apart from being 'able to teach' or 'able to give instruction in sound doctrine and also to rebuke those who contradict it', all the other qualifications demand that all aspiring and serving elders (pastors) not only render a *modicum* of obedience to generic Christian duties, and manifest a *minimum* development of Christian graces, but that they have become *exemplary and blameless* (not sinless) in the fulfillment of these duties and in the embodiment of these graces (1 Tim. 3:1-7; Titus 1:5-9). The little phrase, 'an overseer *must* be' (1 Tim. 3:2), requires such spiritual traits and practices in these office-bearers.

Although Paul insists that every Christian husband *ought* to love his wife as Christ loved the church (Eph. 5:25) and that every Christian father *ought* to take an assertive lead in the nurture of his children (Eph. 6:4), no man may be recognized as an elder who has not attained some degree of evident and exemplary competence in loving his wife and in nurturing his children, assuming he is married and has children. Paul argues that 'if someone does not know how to manage his own household, how will he care for God's church?' (1 Tim. 3:5).

According to these passages there is therefore never any justification for failure to fulfill one's generic Christian duties because of the pressures of specific ministerial responsibilities. In fact, these passages clearly affirm that a man who is not *exemplary* in fulfilling generic Christian duties has no business taking on or continuing in the place of performing specific ministerial duties!

Paul's letter to Titus contains the following scenario. After giving Titus a long and specific list of duties and ethical norms to teach to God's people, Paul counsels Titus that he must be 'in all respects ... a model of good works' (Titus 2:7). The word for 'model' is τύπος (*tupos*), from which our word 'type' is derived. Essentially, Paul is saying, 'Titus, you must strive to be a valid example in your own life of everything that you would incorporate into the lives of those who hear you. When they ask you what this or that Christian duty or grace looks like in real life situations, you should be able to say to them "Be imitators of me, as I am of Christ"' (1 Cor. 11:1). Titus must constantly guard against letting his manifold ministerial responsibilities neutralize his embodiment of all of the generic duties and graces which he preached to the people of God on the isle of Crete.

In his epistle to the Philippians Paul wrote, 'keep your eyes on those who walk according to the example you have in us' (Phil. 3:17). He assumes that among the ordinary members in the assembly at Philippi some believers would be consistent enough in godliness to become valid patterns for other believers. Surely, if this standard is attainable by ordinary believers, it absolutely must be evident in the leaders of Christ's church.

However, the promptings of our indwelling sin are so insidiously subtle, and we are so clever at rationalization, that we often take generic Christian duties one by one and try to suspend them, negate them, or to greatly dilute our performance of them, with feverish attempts to cover such blatant disobedience under the pious guise that attending to our pastoral duties justifies such conduct. If we carry on habitually like this then clearly we are in a backslidden state.

FRUSTRATED WIVES

Let me give a very specific example. Over the years I have met not a few pastors' wives who are some of the most neglected creatures on the face of the earth. The preacher/husband has all kinds of hours to listen to all kinds of problems from all kinds of men and women in the congregation, but he never has even half an hour to let his poor distressed wife sit with him, engage his heart and his ears and pour out her frustrations, her struggles and her spiritual perplexities.

Some of these wives become bitter, deeply frustrated, grieved and wounded because their preacher/husbands have sadly bought the lie that ministering to all their needy sheep, with their frustrations and problems, legitimizes the suspension of their duties and privileges to minister to the needs of their own wives' emotional and spiritual concerns. Are you a man who is excusing his generic duty to love his wife as Christ loves the church, to nurture her as his own body, and to dwell with her in an understanding way – not because you are spending excessive hours on the local golf course, or wasting hours in an undisciplined use of your computer or television? Rather, your time is spent ministering to the needs of your people, and so you experience little disturbance of your conscience relative to the gross neglect of your wife. Without realizing it, you have imbibed the heretical notion that you may legitimately sacrifice your generic Christian duties upon the altar of fulfilling specific ministerial responsibilities.

NEGLECTED CHILDREN

Likewise, some children resent their father's ministry because the ministry has become that ugly and foul thing that robs them of having any meaningful relationship with their dad. A knife pierces their hearts every time they hear the other kids talk about how their dads wrestle on the floor with them, go into the backyard and play ball with them, and how their dads take time to sit and play table games with them, or go hunting and fishing with them, or how their dads help them with their homework and enjoy working on joint projects together. The scriptural imperative is clearly a generic duty laid upon every father, whatever his calling in life may be. It enjoins all, 'Fathers,... bring them up' (Eph. 6:4), without a special indulgence for pastors. But some live as if it were written this way: 'Fathers, bring them up, that is, if you do not happen to be a minister, in which case you are exempt from feeling the direct pressure of this command.'

I am well aware of the words of our Lord Jesus, 'And everyone who has left houses or brothers or sisters or father or mother or children or lands, for my name's sake, will receive a hundredfold and will inherit eternal life' (Matt. 19:29). Unless we are prepared to state that the Bible is full of contradictions, this passage must be referring to circumstances in which these voluntary acts of 'leaving' can be done without in any way disobeying explicit generic Christian duties.

Furthermore, we live in an emergency situation in the overlapping of the ages. Just as there are times when men must leave their domestic sphere to go off to war, or to fulfill business responsibilities, so a man of God may be required to undergo a temporary severance from his domestic context in order to fulfill God-given responsibilities. In these cases no little part of a pastor's wise nurturing of his children will be his tender and patient explanation to them as to why Daddy must leave for a specific period of time. While he is away, his frequent telephone calls and notes to his wife and to his children assure them that he is still their loving and nurturing husband and dad. Furthermore, once home, he will *show* them convincingly that his heart really was with them the whole time he was gone.

I remind my reader of the searching truth recorded in 1 Samuel 15:22-23. There, God speaks the following words to King Saul through the prophetic utterance of Samuel.

And Samuel said, 'Has the LORD as great delight in burnt offerings and sacrifices, as in obeying the voice of the LORD? Behold, to obey is better than sacrifice, and to listen than the fat of rams. For rebellion is as the sin of divination, and presumption is as iniquity and idolatry. Because you have rejected the word of the LORD, he has also rejected you from being king.'

How does God characterize Saul's unwillingness completely to destroy all of the Amalekites, their king, and all of their goods in strict obedience to His revealed will? Not as 'partial obedience', but as blatant rebellion! God regarded such rebellion against His clearly revealed will as an abomination like divination and idolatry.

Here is the fundamental principle. We must never permit specific ministerial duties to be the occasion of negating our generic Christian duties. This was most poignantly illustrated in the life and experience of Dr. Robertson McQuilkin, former president of Columbia Bible College, now Columbia International University. Under Dr. McQuilkin's leadership the school had made significant forward progress in terms of enrollment, facilities and spiritual usefulness. However, his wife began to experience severe dementia. This condition worsened to the point that she was extremely anxious anytime Dr. McQuilkin was not within sight or at her side. In a very moving book entitled 'A Promise Kept' Dr. McQuilkin records the fact that he had no question as to what his duty was. Persuaded that his position as president was an inferred duty, he had no question that loving and nurturing his needy wife was a clearly revealed generic Christian duty. His resignation was submitted.

A PERSONAL TESTIMONY
Coming closer to home, I would share a brief account of my own experience in conjunction with the latter days of my first wife, Marilyn. During her six-year battle with cancer, for

most of that time I was her primary caregiver when special care was needed. I made it plain to her that if she ever became uncomfortable being alone in the house I would relinquish my ministerial responsibilities in order to give myself completely to being with her and caring for her needs. She committed to tell me honestly if and when that time had arrived. Just a little more than one month before the Lord took her to Himself, she very reluctantly made it clear to me that she now felt very fearful whenever I left the house for any length of time. I immediately spoke to my fellow elders, requesting that I be given permission to take an indefinite leave of absence from all of my pastoral responsibilities in order to care for my dying wife. Fulfilling my generic responsibilities to her as a husband was one of the greatest joys and privileges of my Christian life. Marilyn had given herself to me and to the peculiar demands upon my life and family for forty-eight years. I could do nothing less than give myself wholly to serving her in her remaining days. Not for a moment did I ever question that my generic duties to love and nurture her took precedence over any inferred duties connected with the ministry.

May God write upon your heart this very foundational biblical principle that inferred and deduced duties must always yield to duties explicitly revealed. Living out this truth will prove an important means to avoid ministerial backsliding. If you have ignored or grown careless with respect to framing your life by this truth, then coming to grips with it in a fresh way may well become the first step to recovery from a backslidden state.

FOUR

Beware of Trading Off a Good Conscience

I n this chapter we will consider the third warning relative to ministerial backsliding. It is perhaps the most sober warning of all. The warning is this: *Beware of trading off a good conscience before God for proven giftedness and apparent usefulness in the service of God.*

Once again let me begin by explaining my terminology. By a 'good conscience before God', I intend exactly what Paul meant in Acts 24:16 where he said, 'So I always (that is, in the light of the coming day of judgment) take pains to have a clear conscience toward both God and man.' Paul resolved to live with a conscience open to the full light of the law and will of God as revealed in the Scriptures, and that his biblically-enlightened conscience would not justly accuse him, either with matters respecting his relationship to God or to man. This meant that if he were conscious of a sin committed exclusively against God, whether it was a duty omitted or a precept violated, he would go to the fountain opened for sin and for uncleanness and seek forgiveness according to the promise of God in 1 John 1:9. Further, if his sin had been against any fellow man, he would be determined not only to seek the forgiveness of God, but also the forgiveness of the person wronged. Also, if that sin committed at the horizontal level required some tangible restitution, Paul would be prepared to make it in order 'to have a clear conscience toward both God and man.'

Why is living as Paul did in the pursuit of a conscience void of offense such a crucial issue? The apostle himself answers this question in 1 Timothy chapter one, where in verse five he says that one of the major goals for the maintenance of sound doctrine is that of maintaining a good conscience, along with love out of a pure heart, and unfeigned faith. According to this text one of the great ends of God's saving truth is to bring sinners into the state of a good conscience from one that is defiled and accusing.

Tragically, sometimes the following happens to those of us in the ministry. We become aware that we have a controversy with God. It may be what we regard as a 'little thing', or it may be a big thing. For example, in the ministry of last Lord's Day we may have used an autobiographical illustration. Upon reflection we realize that we indulged unjustifiable exaggeration. If we are honest with ourselves, we find conscience speaking clearly to us that we did indeed violate the sanctity of truth (the Ninth Commandment) in order to put ourselves in a better light. We are conscious that we pushed the matter beyond the bounds of any legitimate elasticity with reference to the things we were communicating. To state it bluntly, we told a lie in the pulpit. Conscience smites us in the light of the law of God.

The moment of truth has come. What are we going to do? To have a conscience void of offense toward God, we must humble ourselves and go into His presence through our great Mediator pleading for forgiveness. We will pray frankly something like this: 'O God, to think that in the very context of handling Your Word of truth, and under the special influences of the Spirit of truth attending me in my preaching, I lied!' We then ask God to forgive us for our lying tongue. Our conscience is at rest as we look up into the face of our God and Father. We plead 1 John 1:9 once again and believe that He is indeed 'faithful and just to forgive us our sins and to cleanse us from all unrighteousness.'

But our lie was not just a sin against God. We lied to God's people. Soon Wednesday will come when we must stand before those very same people and give leadership to them as they gather to pray. As we contemplate that reality, our conscience is active once again. We begin to question within ourselves, 'How can I draw near to God within the veil and plead for His blessing upon the life and ministry of the church, when I must do so looking out upon the people to whom I have lied and before whom I have yet to confess my lie?'

Now the warfare begins. You reason within yourself as follows: 'If I confess my lie, what will my people think of me? What will they think of me if I tell them that I lied in the midst of a sermon while preaching the Word of truth? Lord, are You really requiring this of me?' The struggle goes on and another moment of truth arrives. Wednesday evening is upon you. If you would recover a conscience void of offense toward men, you know that the first order of business after the opening hymn is to say to your people, 'Dear brothers and sisters, before we bow in prayer, there is something that I must say to you. If I am to come before God with a good conscience, there is something I must confess to you. In the sermon last Lord's Day morning I said such and such. Upon reflection, I see that that what I said was an exaggeration and alteration of the facts under the impulse of seeking to present myself in a better light. I have sought and received God's forgiveness for this sin. The untainted truth of the matter I related in my sermon is thus and thus. I beg your forgiveness for my sin of lying, and solicit your prayers that in the future I may obey the biblical injunction, "Do not lie to one another".' My dear reader, in the hypothetical situation described, this is the only way to maintain a good conscience, not only toward God, but men.

I have had to make such confessions many times as a resident pastor, since I was 46 years in one place with one congregation. Often, when I have done so, someone would come to me saying essentially, 'Pastor, that must have been a very difficult thing for you to do, confessing your sins before so many people.' My response has always been to tell them that the real difficulty would have been to live with the fruit of my refusal to confess my sin. If I had not confessed my sin I would have grieved the Holy Spirit, suffered an accusing conscience, lost delight in my communion with God and diminished my joy in the Holy Spirit. Neglecting confession also makes it harder not to commit the same sin again, not to mention suffering the experience of Proverbs 28:13, 'Whoever conceals his transgressions will not prosper'.

However, all too often in situations like the one described above, we begin to rationalize. We say to ourselves, 'Well, that really was not such a big thing. Cannot we become overly sensitive? The Bible does talk about an overly-scrupulous conscience, does it not?' We begin to play mind games with ourselves under the influence of our remaining sin. Perhaps you may then go on to say, 'But wait a minute, if the lie were that bad, how is it that even after I spoke it, I was conscious, along with my people, that there was an even greater measure of unction in the latter part of the sermon? So, if the Holy Spirit came upon me with even greater intensity of His felt presence, and upon the people with a shared sense of God's nearness, surely my self-promoting lie could not be that bad.' What have you begun to do? Once again, you have begun to trade off the maintenance of a good conscience for your apparent usefulness in the ministry of the Word. And then, if you refuse to confess your sin to your people at the Wednesday night prayer meeting, and yet the prayer meeting was marked by a copious measure of the Spirit of grace and supplication, you go home Wednesday night even more hardened in your self- deception. Once you have started down that road, where will you find yourself? Having learned the unholy art of trading off a good conscience for proven giftedness and apparent usefulness in the work of God, you have actually put yourself on the high road to serious backsliding and even ultimate apostasy and the destruction of your own soul.

We read in 1 Timothy 1:18-20 words that are frightening, but that speak directly to this issue. The apostle says, 'This charge I entrust to you, Timothy, my child, in accordance with the prophecies previously made about you, that by them you may wage the good warfare, holding faith and a good conscience. By rejecting this (this relative pronoun agrees in number and gender with the word 'conscience') some have made shipwreck of their faith, among whom are Hymenaeus and Alexander, whom I have handed over to Satan that they may learn not to blaspheme.' Paul is saying to his younger colleague in the ministry, 'O Timothy, Timothy, if you are to war a good warfare in the context of your own remaining sin which is constantly injecting its defiling influence into your own soul, hold faith and a good conscience. You must never thrust away a good conscience. It does not matter how many times you may have to humble yourself before the congregation there at Ephesus. It does not matter that you may have to be humbled before your wife and children (if indeed Timothy was married and had children), your fellow workers and the people of God. Timothy, hold to a good conscience as to life itself. Once you have thrust that aside, you are in the path which leads men to spiritual shipwreck.'

Obviously there are going to be a great number on the Day of Judgment who will be exposed as having made a fatal mistake regarding this very issue. Jesus said, 'On that day many will say to me, "Lord, Lord, did we not prophesy in your name, and cast out demons in your name, and do many mighty works in your name?"' (Matt. 7:22). They claimed to have experienced great usefulness in the service of God. Jesus will not debate the validity of their claims, but what *will* He say to them? He will say, 'I never knew you; depart from me, you workers of lawlessness' (Matt. 7:23). Our Lord will go on to remind them that they handled His truth, and were successful in the securing of deliverance for others by means of the truth. However, He will then expose the fact that the truth which was successful to help others when coming out of their mouths was not governing their own hearts and lives because it was obviously not reigning in their own consciences. In spite of all their giftedness and usefulness, they were still 'workers of lawlessness'.

How much backsliding and even ultimate apostasy begins in the ministry when we start trading off a good conscience before God for apparent giftedness and usefulness in the service of God! It may all begin with something as 'little' as the hypothetical incident of a 'pulpit lie'. However, once the conscience is defiled because of a refusal to confess our sin to God, and where necessary to men, frightening declension begins to set in. A defiled and an accusing conscience makes us indisposed to have close dealings with God and His Word. After that, it is no wonder that on Thursday morning after the Wednesday prayer meeting (back to the hypothetical 'pulpit lie'), instead of going immediately to the place where you ordinarily pray, you suddenly begin to think of all the unanswered telephone calls and e-mails that have accumulated during the past several days. You rationalize that if you are going to pray and keep your mind on the Lord, that you must get those phone calls out of the way. When they are all out of the way, and you start to go to the place of prayer, your mind turns to the several unanswered letters that remain on your desk. You rationalize that your testimony will be jeopardized if you do not get those letters written or dictated in a timely fashion. The letters get dictated or sent out on your computer, and now it is almost near noon and you say to yourself, 'Well, it is close to lunch time. I will pray after lunch.' Then, after lunch, you say to yourself, 'This is the worst time of the day to pray. It is my dopey time. I would dishonor God by coming with the broken legs and crippled arms of a dull and distracted mind and insult God with such kinds of prayers. I will make several pastoral calls, and then when my mind is more alert, I will give myself to prayer.' Brethren, is this all fantasy? No, it is not. This is exactly what happens when we have a controversy with God in the realm of conscience. There is an indisposition to pray that in turn makes us indisposed to be watchful. We are now vulnerable to our specific areas of weakness, perhaps with respect to sins that have not troubled us for months or even years. Perhaps it is the lust of the eyes, and on your way to make a hospital call ostensibly in the name of Christ, your eyes lingered where they ought not. Having further defiled your conscience, and created an even greater indisposition to having heart dealings with God, you have, without realizing it, placed yourself on that dangerous downward spiral slide into a backslidden condition that can eventually lead to apostasy.

Need I go on to describe the sordid process of declension? Ministerial backsliding is indeed a horrible and frightening reality. Some of us have lived long enough to see the pathway of Christian profession and ministerial usefulness strewn with the terrifying and grotesquely-twisted wreckage resulting from the toleration of the first signs of ministerial backsliding. One of the problems is that our people do not have the luxury we do of trading off a good conscience for apparent giftedness and usefulness in the house of God. What a tragic thing it would be if our gifts and our usefulness should be the occasion of our damnation. Far better for God to allow our tongues to be ripped from our mouths than to let us go on thinking that because we speak in His name, speak well and with apparent success, that we must not take too seriously our sins and deal with them in such a way as 'to have a clear conscience toward both God and man'.

Listen to the sagacious and searching words of John Owen who, as few others, seems to be able to dive into the depths of the human heart, and not only discover what is there, but to articulate that discovery with penetrating precision. Owen wrote:

> I am persuaded that there are very few that apostatize from a profession of any continuance, such as our days abound withal, but their door of entrance into the folly of backsliding was either some great and notorious sin that bloodied their consciences, tainted their affections, and intercepted all delight of having anything more to do with God; or else it was a course of neglect in private duties, arising from a weariness of contending against that powerful aversation which they found in themselves unto them.[1]

The Scriptures inform us that 'the desires of the flesh are against the Spirit, and the desires of the Spirit are against the flesh' (Gal. 5:17). Owen has reminded us of the fact that when men grow weary of contending with this constant tendency to rationalize our sin, this constant tendency to justify our sin, this constant tendency to avoid close and honest dealings with God regarding our sin, it is then that some enter the door that eventually leads into their very apostasy.

Oh, that God would help us to lay this warning to heart! Let us avoid ministerial backsliding by being determined that we will never *trade off a good conscience before God because of proven giftedness and apparent usefulness in the service of God.*

---

1 'Remainders of Indwelling Sin in Believers', *The Works of John Owen*, VI, p. 184.

FIVE

Beware of Losing Your Own Nurture by Isolation from the Congregation

In this fourth warning concerning ministerial backsliding I want to address something omitted from most of the books I have read which in any way address the subject of ministerial backsliding. Its omission both surprises and grieves me. I suspect it is not addressed because it is either assumed to be so self-evident as to need no mention, or else it is a reflection of an incipient clericalism that negates a very vital truth of Scripture. This is my fourth warning: *Beware of allowing the position and duties of the ministry to isolate you from the nurture of the body of Christ within which you serve as a special gift of Christ.*

Ephesians 4:1-16 is the foundational text which sets the framework for this concern. Here the apostle Paul states that within the one body, indwelt by the one Spirit and submissive to the one

Lord, there are diversities of gifts. Identifying some of these gifts, he affirms that the ascended Christ gives 'the shepherds and teachers, to equip the saints for the work of ministry, for building up the body of Christ' (v. 12). He concludes this section of the Word of God with that marvelous picture of the body building up itself through that which every joint supplies, and growing up into the fullness of the stature of Christ in a context of love. Assumed in all of that teaching is the fact that though pastors and teachers are given to the church for a specific and prominent function within the body, they are not exempt from an organic connection to the body. Therefore these pastors and teachers, like all the other members of the body, are also dependent upon the nourishment which comes through the other parts of the body.

The picture in this passage is one in which the body is envisioned as being brought to maturity 'by every joint with which it is equipped' (Eph. 4:16). The entire body ministers to itself. Granted, as pastors we have a high profile and more prominent sphere of public influence in that process of maturation, but by what kind of biblical reasoning can we come to the conclusion that, for all intents and purposes, we do not need intimate spiritual and organic interaction with the body for the well-being of our own souls? I see nothing in the Bible that points us in that direction. Even the great apostle Paul, a mature and seasoned saint, desired to visit the church at Rome for the end of *mutual* edification, including that they might contribute something to him (Rom. 1:10-12).

Acts 20:28 is another text that will help us to think biblically concerning this fourth warning. There we learn that the elders of the church at Ephesus were given a solemn and distinct responsibility to care for the flock of God in that city. However, the language in which Paul expresses this responsibility is very precise. 'Pay careful attention to yourselves and to all the flock, *in which* the Holy Spirit has made you overseers, to care for the church of God, which he obtained with his own blood.' While the KJV has, '*over* the which the Holy Ghost hath made you overseers', the preposition 'over' is better rendered 'wherein' (Gk. ɛv), stressing the elders' being *within* the church. While Paul does not downplay the distinct and high profile responsibilities of these elders, he wants them to understand that all of their labors are to be carried on as men who themselves are 'within the flock'.

These perspectives from Ephesians 4 and Acts 20 are critical. If we view ourselves in our official duties and position as not needing the ministry of the body to ourselves, we will have put ourselves in the way of ministerial backsliding because we have, for all intents and purposes, negated one of the primary means God Himself has established for our spiritual maturation. Our growth into the fullness of the stature of Christ does not come simply or exclusively as we meet with our fellow elders, with ministerial friends or any local presbytery or ministerial fraternal. We must look upon and interact with our people biblically. We must view ourselves biblically when we stand before them to preach the Word, recognizing that the Holy Spirit has constituted us overseers among them and that we have a solemn responsibility to shepherd them. But when we are out of the pulpit and not engaged in individual pastoral ministry we are primarily members of the body who need what that body can contribute to us. Merely interacting with our people, we are nobody special.

Do we seize every opportunity to mingle with our people both frequently and freely? Do we ask our brethren the questions that make it evident that we are ready to be taught by them? For example, think of that faithful man with the gnarly mechanic's hands, with grease under his fingernails and with a rather limited formal education. He has learned how to maintain communion with God in the midst of a cursing, swearing, and noise-filled environment. Day by day he must walk by indecent centerfolds hung up on the walls of the shop where he works. Does he not have something to teach us about how to maintain a godly mindset in an ungodly context? He may know much more about this than we do. Do we ever ask him to teach us?

Take that dear woman, harassed with 'mommy this and mommy that' all day long, with four children all under five years of age. Yet there is serenity, a beautiful dignity, almost a halo of divine peace and glory upon her countenance. You see it when you preach. You would think she was an evangelical nun who had just stepped out of the rigidly structured life in a convent! She sits under the preaching of the Word utterly undistracted. Her face is turned upward to you as you minister the Word of God. She is evidently wrapped up in God and His truth. Do you ever go to her and say, 'My dear sister, I have only a little idea what your world is like, but it is evident that when you come into the house of God and you are among the people of God, somehow, you are able to put all those things behind you. Would you please tell me your secret?' My brother, do you really believe that those supposedly insignificant members have something to contribute to you? Put yourself in the place where they can minister to you or you may well be despising a vital means of grace mediated through Christ's body, the church. If that happens, you will backslide as surely as you would if you were chronically neglecting the devotional assimilation of the Word of God.

Certainly, whatever our particular ecclesiology may be in terms of a two- or three-office theory of church officers,[1] this much is true: there is no one envisioned in the New Testament who as a Christian is to be without bona fide accountability to the Body of Christ, and that suggests interaction with others. If even Paul was not a freelance Christian, how can we afford to be? No sooner was he converted, baptized and filled with the Holy Spirit, but we read that 'for some days he was *with the disciples* at Damascus' (Acts 9:19). Then, when persecution

---

1   Historically, the two-office view asserts that the only officers recognized in the New Testament are elders and deacons. The three-office view asserts that the preaching and teaching minister (elder) constitutes a separate office from that of ruling elders.

drove him out of Damascus, he ended up in Jerusalem. The first thing he attempted to do was '*to join* the disciples' (Acts 9:26). At first the disciples were suspicious of him. However, through the intervention of Barnabas, God's saints in Jerusalem were persuaded that Paul was indeed a true Christian. He was welcomed into the Jerusalem church. The Scriptures tell us that as a result of that relationship, 'he went in and out *among them* at Jerusalem' (Acts 9:28).

I ask you, my brother, do you have any real accountability with your fellow elders and other church officers? If you lack fellow elders, have you singled out some men who truly know and walk with God, who love you enough to be brutally honest with you, and made yourself accountable to them? Do you really move among your people anxious to learn from them, and where appropriate, to be questioned or reproved by them? When is the last time anyone lovingly and yet pointedly felt free to ask you, 'Pastor, how is your devotional life?' If they were to do this, would you stiffen and respond by saying, 'Who are you to ask me?'

Many years ago a young woman was brought into the membership at Trinity Baptist Church when I was still one of the pastors. After a short period of time I inquired as to how she was settling into the life of the church. She responded that she was doing quite well. She then went on recount something that at the time shocked her. I inquired as to what that was. She said that she had not been long in the membership when one of her sisters in the church came up to her and inquired of her concerning the state of her devotional life. This woman told me that she felt like saying to the inquirer, 'That is none of your business.' She then went on to recount to me the fact that she had been in various evangelical churches for more than 20 years and that no one had ever asked her such a question. What a shame! Members one of another, and yet no communication concerning the things that are most valued and important. It is a double shame when you as a pastor, one with access to the affections and the esteem of your people, do not use this relationship as a means for your spiritual advancement.

Do you have that kind of mutual respect and love among your fellow elders that you can call one another to account where necessary? Can you lovingly point out one another's sins? While in the posture of assuming the best, can you ask questions of one another that may uncover the worst? A number of years ago I was sitting with my fellow elders in a regular weekly elders' meeting. We were discussing the fact that a pastor in our circles had recently been exposed as a man who was addicted to Internet pornography. In that setting, knowing that some of my fellow elders had computers and were using the Internet, I solemnly charged each of my fellow pastors to answer with Judgment Day honesty the following question: 'Are you in any way dabbling with Internet pornography?' One brother responded by saying, 'I knew you would ask this question of all of us, and I am thankful. I have been struggling with this very issue, and I am grateful for the opportunity to get it out in the open where it can be dealt with.' Thankfully, after careful questioning of the nature and extent of this brother's involvement with pornography, the entire eldership was of one mind that the issue could be dealt with by repentance and accountability in such a way that public exposure and the relinquishment of his office was not a biblical necessity, although the man was willing for both if his fellow elders judged such were necessary. Ongoing accountability has confirmed that the brother has been able to mortify that sin by the power of the Holy Spirit.

Beware, my brethren, of allowing the position and duties of the ministry to isolate you from the nurture of the body of Christ in which you serve. You need real accountability, real spiritual interaction with the flock and a practical relationship within which you are prepared to learn from them.

Permit me to share a personal anecdote which I trust will underscore this fourth warning. During the conference at which these lectures/sermons were originally given, I was privileged to preach at one of the evening public meetings. At the conclusion of one such meeting one of the young men as he was leaving took my hand and said to me words to this effect.

> Pastor, I am no officer in this church. At this point in my life, I do not have any aspiration to any church office. But I want to say that sitting under the Word tonight, the Holy Spirit was unusually present, ministering to my own mind and heart. I was brought to see as I have never seen before the commitment that those of you who have gone before us have had and what the truths are that you have given yourselves to – truths that have molded and shaped this place that has been a haven for my wife and for me in the process of our spiritual maturation. I want to tell you, pastor, I am ready by the grace of God to spend and be spent and spill my blood so that my children will have the same legacy.

My brethren in the ministry, you will not get that kind of input from your people if you are a distant and detached Reverend! Place yourselves among the flock – physically, emotionally and spiritually, so that it is evident to them that you look to them for their input as a vital aspect of your own growth in grace and ongoing conformity to Christ. I am convinced that many men are deeply discouraged in the ministry because they have created a climate in which it never occurs to their people that they need any encouragement from them. They never say as Paul did, 'But God, who comforts the downcast, comforted us by the coming of Titus' (2 Cor. 7:6). Paul acknowledges that on a given day he was in the dumps and was lonely. You say, 'An apostle in the dumps and lonely?' Yes. 'Fighting without and fear within' (7:5). Oh my brother, dismantle every bit of that wretched wall of clericalism that cuts you off from real edifying interaction with your people! Pray that the Spirit of God will come like a consuming fire and burn up that clerical cocoon within which you hide yourself from your people. It is when we freely acknowledge among our people that we are 'men of

51

like passions' with them that they will feel free to relate to us in a way that makes their interaction a means of grace to us.

As a younger pastor I functioned under the restrictions of a false notion that in great measure cut me off from the sanctifying influence of the body of Christ in which I ministered. It was the notion that a pastor must have no close personal friends drawn from the flock of God in which he serves as an under-shepherd. I had absorbed this notion from the climate of the broad Evangelicalism which was the context of my nurture as a young believer. Thankfully, God subsequently graciously used a fellow elder to purge that notion from me and free my conscience to pursue the establishment of some close friendships within the flock of God.

God Incarnate was unashamed to make it known that among the Twelve He had three special friends. Furthermore, He made it evident that among the three, He had one very special friend. Given the clear revelation of these facts in the Gospel records, no one who believes in the authority of Scripture can rationally argue with these facts. Our Lord showed the kind of 'favoritism' connected with the establishment of special friendships. Some might object, 'But will not this leave others vulnerable to jealousy?' Yes, it will. In fact, it did in the case of our blessed Lord. However, He still cultivated those deliberately selective closer friendships. Our Lord made such friendships and kept them no secret. When it was appropriate, He openly and unashamedly took Peter, James and John with Him into situations, such as when they were with Him on the Mount of Transfiguration. Those three were taken into a deeper fellowship with Him in the Garden of Gethsemane. John, the object of His most special friendship love, was privileged to be found 'at Jesus' side' (John 13:23). Since the Scriptures tell us that 'whoever says he abides in him ought to walk in the same way in which he walked' (1 John 2:6), we ought to pursue these more intimate friendships within the flock of God.

I trust you have been persuaded that this fourth warning against ministerial backsliding and burnout is indeed a much needed warning. *Beware of allowing the position and duties of the ministry to isolate you from the nurture of the body of Christ in which you serve as an under-shepherd and overseer.*

CLOSING PRAYER

Father, as we have turned our attention to those peculiar ways in which the devil and our indwelling sin can ensnare us in the very course of seeking to be your servants, we confess that it has not been pleasant for us to look into our own hearts. What we see of our almost infinite capacity to deceive ourselves and to leave ourselves vulnerable shocks us. Lord, it scares us. When we hear you say, 'Therefore let anyone who thinks that he stands take heed lest he fall,' we cry out, 'O God have mercy upon us lest we fall!'

We thank You for Your Word that says You are the One who is able to keep us from falling and to present us faultless before Your presence with exceeding joy. We pray that by the Word and the Spirit these principles would be so written upon our hearts and become regulative of our conduct, that we may not only be preserved from ministerial backsliding and ministerial burnout, but that we may go from strength to strength and that by Your grace we may continue to make progress – progress that is evident to all. May we, in the language of Your own Word, be men who are full of sap and green even to old age. O God, deliver us from ministerial brittleness and dryness and fruitless ministries in which we say the same things with the same or even increasing precision of orthodoxy, but say them without feeling, without warmth, and without a present felt enjoyment of them.

O God, have mercy upon us! Look upon us with pity in all of our unusual vulnerability as Your servants. Deliver us and keep us for Your glory and for the good of Your church. We thank You again for the privilege of meeting together. We thank You for the privilege which will now be ours of sitting together about the tables ministering one to another. Lord, give us a disposition that will make us truly open to the ministry of our brethren. We thank You again for calling us together for these days. Continue with us, we plead, as we offer our prayers and thanksgiving for all of Your mercies through our Lord Jesus Christ. Amen.

WARNINGS

AGAINST

MINISTERIAL BURNOUT

Six

Beware of Priorities Shaped by Others' Perceived Needs

Opening Prayer:

Our Father, we are deeply grateful for the pervasive sense of Your presence with us and Your grace upon us in these days. We confess that we are both thankful and humbled whenever You are pleased to draw near to us and to give us a measure of grace to feel spiritual realities. We plead that this day will be no exception to that blessed reality.

We thank You that as a loving Father You know our frame, and You remember that we are dust. You know that days such as these marked by sustained, concentrated, mental and spiritual discipline and exercise of heart take their toll upon our frail humanity. We beg of You that You would give us unusual measures of mental, spiritual and emotional alertness and quickening. We ask this, not simply that we may feel and enjoy spiritual realities, but, O God, that we may grasp them and absorb them, and by Your Spirit's grace and power hide them in our hearts for the days to come.

Send Your Spirit and fulfill Your promise. 'They who wait for the LORD shall renew their strength; they shall mount up with wings like eagles; they shall run and not be weary; they shall walk and not faint.' Lord, we believe this promise comes sealed to us in the blood of Your beloved Son, and we hold it up before You. Please make it good in our midst today. We ask these mercies for the sake and honor of the Lord Jesus Christ, and in His name. Amen.

In this chapter we will consider the fifth warning against ministerial backsliding and burnout. This particular warning relates primarily, if not exclusively, to ministerial burnout. The warning is this: *beware of allowing the use of your time and the proportions of your pastoral labors to be dictated by the perceived needs of your people.*

First of all let me describe the situations I have in mind and then I will seek to give the practical antidote. If, under God, you develop a relationship with your people that to any degree approximates the biblical concept of the relationship between a shepherd and his sheep, it will not be long before you will have a demanding ministry in what is currently described as 'pastoral counseling'. For a number of reasons I prefer the expression, 'individual pastoral care'. This aspect of pastoral duty and privilege could, in many situations, totally absorb almost all of your time. This possibility is a peculiarly intensified danger if we are called upon to minister in a context where there has been a widespread erosion of God's common grace in the experience of any society. Those of us who minister in Western society at the beginning of the twenty-first century are ministering in a context where a massive erosion of common grace has occurred. Others who read these pages may be called upon to minister in societies where there has never been any widespread influence of the Gospel, and therefore there is little of the leavening influence of common grace in the fabric of that society.

For example, there has been a tragic erosion of the nuclear family functioning with some degree of normalcy according to biblical standards. It is increasingly rare to find non-Christian families comprised of a strong male leader conducting himself as a discerning, loving husband and father joined with a truly feminine, domestically-oriented woman functioning as a supportive wife and a stay-at-home nurturing mother. Increasingly rare in our society is the family that is comprised of children who are lovingly disciplined and reared in a climate in which they are taught the dynamics of healthy interpersonal relationships under the strict scrutiny of an assertive and loving father and a supportive and nurturing mother.

To demonstrate how extensive this erosion has been let me give you some personal reminiscences. I was born in 1934. I would take you back to Stamford, Connecticut in the late 1930s and the early 1940s. The immediate neighborhood in which we lived was like the UN. There was what we affectionately described as a little Italy. We had a little Ireland. There was also a little Poland. There was one apartment dwelling on our street which housed a very pronounced Scottish man who was exceedingly proud of his Scottish accent and background. To my knowledge there were no Christians in any of those families, with perhaps one exception. However, there was at least a semblance of the structure of family life that I have just described. There were no single-parent homes. There were no wives and mothers working outside the home, with but one exception. That meant that within all of those families there was, in common grace, a climate that put tremendous wholesome pressure upon all of the children being reared by the families in that neighborhood. All of the parents assumed that the other parents would be honest about the conduct of their children. So if Mrs. Yates, the Irishwoman across the street from our home, told my parents that I had gotten into a fight with her son, or that I had used some curse words, my parents assumed that her allegations were true. I would then be brought into my 'family court' and by one means or another the truth would be drawn out of me. Once the truth was established I would be disciplined for trying to avoid the truth, and then disciplined for the truth discovered. If my parents saw some undesirable behavior in Mrs. Yates son's life that warranted communication with his parents, there was an equally valid exchange of neighborhood information.

More recollections. There was a small grocery store in our immediate neighborhood. If the owner and proprietor said to any of the parents in the area that their child was trying to steal some of the candy from the candy rack, the parents assumed that the proprietor was being honest. If we had been guilty of this crime we would then be marched back to the store to confess our crime and to make restitution. The same proprietor of the grocery store would grant food on credit (credit cards were nonexistent), assuming that the neighbors would pay their bill as soon as they were able to do so. That is the world in which I lived and grew up, and that was not something unusual. That was Middle America at that stage of our national life. There was no television to bombard our minds with images and concepts antithetical to biblical norms. There were no Walkman CD players, no MP3 players, no iPods, etc., to din into our ears every day the lawless and often vile lyrics of rock groups. There was no readily-available pornography, whether in magazines or on the Internet. These few details of my memories should convince any thoughtful reader that there has indeed been nothing short of a massive erosion of common grace in our society.

Along with this massive erosion of common grace, particularly manifested in family structures, is the tragic fact that the Bible has been pushed out to the very fringes of our society. Biblical illiteracy is the order of the day.

As a result of these tragic realities, when the Lord is pleased to save men and women out of this present society, they come to us with all the fundamental needs of both spiritual and generic nurture. They come into our churches in desperate need of being re-parented from the diaper stage upward. They have not been taught those very fundamental things which are essential to a well-ordered, disciplined and productive life. They have not been taught respect for and submission to constituted authority. They have not been taught fiscal responsibility. They have not been taught the judicious use of time. They lack many of the things that God has ordained should be learned in a home where there is an assertive, loving, dominant man functioning as father and husband, along with a supportive, feminine, domestic woman functioning as wife and mother. They lack the molding influence of a two-parent family in which both mother and father are constantly engaged in the character development of their children – a family in which there is constant cultivation of basic social graces and conflict resolution by means of parental monitoring of sibling interaction. They have neither seen nor experienced the wholesome influence that is the fruit of reinforcing patterns of conduct with consistent and reasonable rewards and discipline. People come to us with little, if any, of the kind of positive character-shaping input that is fundamentally a parental and domestic responsibility.

When God regenerates such people they are brought to repentance and faith. In the complex of conversion they are given the Spirit of adoption and they are united to Christ. Now they are endowed with both motivation and power to grow into the kind of people God wants them to be. Of them it may be said, 'it is God who works in you, both to will and to work for his good pleasure' (Phil. 2:13). However, God does not have a special packet of all those graces and disciplines and perspectives of general life skills which He stuffs into their psyches on the occasion of their conversion. That just does not happen. What happens when such people are converted and brought into our churches? We pastors end up not only seeking to establish the new converts in the basic truths of the Gospel and the practical issues that are addressed in the Word of God, but in many ways we have to become fathers to them. We must give ourselves to helping them in the massive task of catching up on all the fundamental life skills essential to responsible living. In many situations it is proper that we give a modicum of these fatherly directives by means of individual pastoral care.

But now that their hearts have embraced biblical norms, including principled submission to constituted authority and the benefits that come from that submission, they latch on to their pastors and begin to view them as surrogate fathers. They may begin to expect, and even subtly demand, that we relate to them in that way, as though we were responsible to train them from diapers to adulthood. When this happens one may be inundated with the pressures of individual pastoral care that arise from this need for parenting as well as pastoring. If we allow the perceived needs of such people to dictate the apportionment of our time and labor, it will not be long before we will be suffering classic ministerial burnout.

We will be plagued with a guilty conscience that we are not really spending the time in sermon preparation that we ought to spend so as to be confident when we stand to preach that we are indeed 'rightly handling the word of truth' (2 Tim. 2:15). We are conscious that we are not engaging in the kind of general reading that is calculated to keep our minds fresh and healthy, in good overall mental resilience, so that when we come to specific sermon preparation, our mental faculties are in their best shape. As a result we carry about a guilty conscience that we are failing in this explicit responsibility to preach the Word and to feed the flock of God.

On the other hand, as we seek to preserve the disciplines essential to a vigorous and faithful pulpit ministry, we end up with a guilty conscience that we are not adequately caring for the bleating sheep with desperate needs, limping and halting because of their inability to function to the glory of God in specific areas of their lives. Some of these bleating sheep are men who don't know how to sort out and exercise authoritative, dominant male leadership in the spirit of humility, tenderness, vulnerability,and manifested love. Many men have never seen such leadership. They do not know what it looks like in the concrete and specific details of life, so they are crying out for hands-on pastoral help in this area. Furthermore, others desperately need to be helped in biblically cultivating wholesome and godly career ambition. We cannot possibly respond to all those needs. We feel guilty for not meeting the needs of our sheep. So to relieve our guilt feelings, what do we do? We start spending more and more time with these needy sheep. Then we once more begin to feel guilt that we are falling short of being competent preachers. After a while, this ping-pong, double-guilt scenario leads to depression, until a man may even doubt the validity of his call and wonder if he is indeed in the right place seeking to minister as an under-shepherd.[1]

What has happened? In many cases we have allowed the use of our time and the proportion of our pastoral labors to be dictated by the perceived needs of our people. I recall a tragic example of this scenario leading to ministerial burnout – an example with which I was personally acquainted. A man began to give up his planned exercise times and to schedule counseling sessions in their place. He felt guilty whenever he had a free evening where he would just sit and read a wholesome novel or watch a ballgame on television. He began to say to himself, 'If I am really sold out to Christ and if I truly love my people, I will be found among the sheep every evening of the week.' And what happened? The last I knew, he was not preaching any

---

1 Cf. 'The Church Ministering to Itself in Love' (MI-MB-78 and MI-MB-79), available from The Trinity Pulpit ministry of Trinity Baptist Church, Montville, New Jersey. This is a subject that I seek to address in some detail in my Pastoral Theology Lectures, now professionally recorded and packaged in DVD format. This subject is dealt with in Unit 7, Lecture #6. Each of the eight units may be purchased separately from the Trinity Pulpit. Information is available at: www.trinitymontville.org

sermons to anyone. He was not ministering in any way to any of God's needy sheep. Burnout. Breakdown. Why? For the very reason that he allowed the use and apportionment of his time to be dictated by the perceived needs of his people.

The antidote to these patterns leading to ministerial burnout is found, in principle, in three texts of Scripture that I would set before you.

The priority of the Master

The first is Mark 1:35-39. Here is the example of our Lord Jesus Christ, who did not, as a general rule, apportion His time, energy, and activities by others' perceived needs. A higher authority controlled how our Lord managed His time and expended His energies. In this particular passage we read that our Lord had been up late the previous evening giving Himself to healing the sick and casting out demons. In verse 35 it says, 'And rising very early in the morning, while it was still dark, he departed and went out to a desolate place, and there he prayed.' Upon waking that morning He knew He needed a season of intense and protracted waiting upon and communing with His heavenly Father. Hence the Lord Jesus rose early and went out to a desert place for concentrated prayer. However, soon after He left the house and went into the desert, 'Simon and those who were with him searched for him, and they found him.' The telephone could not get to Him but His disciples could. It took a little longer; feet do not move as fast as electrical impulses. Therefore His season of solitude was interrupted. His disciples, having found Him, said to Him 'Everyone is looking for you.' Could it be that their appeal went something like this? 'Lord, we have just come from a place where the physical and spiritual needs of men and women were not all met, even though You gave Yourself to meeting those needs into the night hours of yesterday. The people in the very town where You ministered so selflessly are seeking for You. Lord, should You not return to minister to these who desperately need and earnestly desire Your ministry?'

The text gives no indication that these people who were seeking our Lord were motivated by merely desiring to look on the famous preacher and obtain His autograph. Sick, demon-possessed people were seeking Him for His healing touch. People who were spiritually whipped and scourged by the wretched teachings and practices of the Pharisee were longing to hear His liberating and life-giving words. One can only imagine something of the tremendous pull this report exerted upon the holy, loving soul of the Son of God when Peter said, 'Everyone is looking for you.'

What did our Lord do? He steeled Himself against the holy, reflexive impulses of His own soul. Compassion, desire to meet human needs, and actions calculated to meet those needs were the normal reactions of incarnate love. Yet He said to the disciples, 'Let us go on to the next towns, that I may preach there also, for that is why I came out.' Jesus was saying that He would not allow the needs of men, expressed with tremendous intensity and in such a way as to move His heart of compassion, to determine how He would apportion His time and expend His energy. It was the revealed will of His Father that determined such things. He knew that the mission on which He was sent did not allow Him more days in that town in which He had ministered the day before. The holy Son of God, while possessed of holy emotions that no doubt pressured Him to go back into that town, nevertheless steeled Himself and said 'no'. Had He responded to the perceived needs of the people in that town in the way that they desired, He would have been ministering (may I say it reverently) to needy men and women at the expense of doing the clearly-revealed will of God.

My pastor-brother, there may well be times when you are sitting in your study ministering to the perceived needs of a needy sheep or engaged in other activities in response to the perceived needs of men and women at the expense of doing the clearly-revealed will of God in connection with other pastoral responsibilities that minister to the needs of the whole flock of God.

JESUS AND MARY AND MARTHA

A second passage to which I direct your attention is John chapter 11. The context of our Lord's actions here is not one in which He is confronted with generic masses of nameless people. Whenever He saw needy multitudes, He 'had compassion on them' (Mark 6:34). But here in John 11, we find our Lord in the presence of what was probably His most intimate circle of domestic friendships revealed in the Scriptures. The text says:

> Now a certain man was ill, Lazarus of Bethany, the village of Mary and her sister Martha. It was Mary who anointed the Lord with ointment and wiped his feet with her hair, whose brother Lazarus was ill. So the sisters sent to him, saying, 'Lord, he whom you love is ill.'

The sisters knew how to touch the heart of our Lord. They did not say, 'Behold, Lazarus is sick,' but they reminded our Lord that Lazarus was the object of His particular love. They are saying in essence, 'Lord, everything in our previous interaction with You indicates that You have a particular attachment to our brother Lazarus in human affection, as well as in divine and redemptive love. He to whom You are bound in these unique cords of love is sick.' This was a far more powerful appeal than simply asking if Jesus would come and heal Lazarus. John goes on to tell us that:

> But when Jesus heard it he said, 'This illness does not lead to death. It is for the glory of God, so that the Son of God may be glorified through it.' Now Jesus loved Martha and her sister and Lazarus (vv. 4-5).

The compelling influence of the perceived need of Mary and Martha is heightened by John reminding us that Jesus not only loved Lazarus, but had a special affection for Martha and her sister Mary as well. But then we have a very strange verse in the ongoing narrative. John records the following: 'So, when he (Jesus) heard that Lazarus was ill, he stayed two days longer in the place where he was' (v. 6).

Having been apprised of the great need in the household at Bethany, our Lord does the exact opposite of what we think that love would do. Rather than rushing to heal Lazarus, Jesus stays on for two days in the place where He was. He was prepared to give the impression of a measure of hardheartedness and indifference to His intimate friends. Obviously that impression took hold and was expressed in the mild rebuke that one of the sisters later gave Him. She said to Jesus, 'Lord, if you had been here, my brother would not have died' (v. 21). In other words, she is charging Him with a measure of indifference to the gravity of their need. She is saying in essence, 'You did not care enough to come when we sent the message concerning our brother's sickness. There was enough time for You to get here. You have disappointed us, Lord.' Jesus deliberately exposed Himself to the temporary impression of hardheartedness for the ultimate good of the very ones upon whom that impression was made.

The sisters were asking Jesus to come in order to heal their brother, but Jesus had a more glorious end in view – raising Lazarus from the dead! Now what is the vital principle embedded in this passage? The principle is this: We do not claim to have the same kind of relationship with God that Jesus had, one which involved the revelation of the will of God within the orbit of the unique interpersonal relationships of the members of the Godhead. Yet by means of a careful and prayerful consideration of the broad principles and the specific precepts of the Word of God, we must order our time and our energies according to the revealed will of God. We must resist the pull of our deepest affections to Christ's sheep and their expressed needs to dictate how we will manage our time and energy. We must expose ourselves to the suspicion of being hardhearted at times when people think they know how best we can respond to their needs. If you want to be faithful to your calling and avoid ministerial burnout you must be willing to serve your Master in the way that He rendered service to His heavenly

Father. Our blessed Lord was able to say in every situation, 'I always do the things that are pleasing to him' (John 8:29).

Now remember, these actions of Jesus did not occur at the beginning of His forging that unique friendship with Lazarus, Mary and Martha. This is why in their disappointment they did not come to our Lord and say, 'By waiting to come to us You have negated all that You have previously conveyed to us concerning Your special love for us and our brother.' No, there was just a mild word of irritation and disappointment: 'Lord, if you had been here, my brother would not have died.' Here is a great lesson. When you establish intimate, open-faced, loving bonds with your people, those bonds can stand the strain of an occasional impression that you really do not love them. Eventually they will see that what you did was really the highest dictate of love.

Let me illustrate this principle with a specific incident from my pastoral experience. Years ago in the course of my ministry at Trinity Baptist Church, God began to give us some significant inroads into the Black community in our area. How God did this is a marvelous story reflecting God's mysterious and wonderful sovereignty in the building of His church. About that time Bill Moyer's documentary focusing on the Black experience in the city of Newark was released on public television. I took time to view it and then spoke to one of our responsible Black brothers in the church, asking if he had seen the documentary. He told me he had indeed watched it. I had it taped and was going to gather our Black brothers and sisters from the Newark area and ask them to evaluate the accuracy of that documentary. This particular brother affirmed without reservation how accurate that documentary was. In fact, he told me that the man who was shown as one of the 'local studs' who had fathered five or six children did not presently live with any one of the women whose children he fathered. He told me that he knew that particular man by name. Further, he said that the young woman, who was featured in the film as a junkie and the mother of two or three children, was now dead. As a kind of summary statement he said to me, 'The Newark portrayed in that documentary is the Newark in which I was reared.'

Among those from the Black community who were beginning to come into the membership of Trinity Baptist Church, there was a young couple who were brought up in the Newark area. Their marriage was in shambles, held together by a thread so thin that only the Lord could see it. They were grossly ignorant of the most fundamental issues relative to a stable marriage and a well-ordered family life. What is the role of a husband and father? What is the role of a wife and a mother? What are the biblical patterns for a godly marital relationship? What is the biblical perspective on career ambition? At every level they needed someone to function as a father bringing them into responsible adult and Christian behavior. We sought to take them where they were, spending concentrated hours with them in individual pastoral care, in addition to the input of the public ministry of the Word of God which was giving them some basic understanding of these issues.

One does not become this deeply involved in the lives of true Christians without developing some very strong bonds of felt mutual affection. I began to sense that the young man was adopting me more and more into the role of a father. Whenever he had to make a decision he would call me for my input. Our relationship developed to the place where he even asked me if he could call me 'Dad'. At some point I decided that he now had grasped enough of the general principles of the Word of God to begin to make decisions on his own. I was convinced that to some degree his own spiritual muscles would not develop as they should unless he began learning to walk on his own. I perceived that he needed in some measure to be weaned from me.

Situations like this underscore the benefits of taking all your calls through an answering machine with the monitor on. I would hear his voice on the answering machine monitor saying something like this, 'Pastor, I must talk to you. I have a decision to make this afternoon by five o'clock and I am just not ready to make it.' I would sit at my desk assuming my 'hardhearted posture'. I would not pick up the phone. I did not call him back. I would wait two or three days. Then when I would see him at prayer meeting or on the Lord's Day I would take him aside and say something along these lines. 'I got your call on Monday. I deliberately did not pick up the phone. I wanted you to learn how to be exercised in making wise decisions without my input. How did that situation work out?' On one occasion his response was something like this: 'Oh, Pastor, when I could not get to you, it drove me to my knees and into my Bible. God gave me wisdom and the issue has been completely resolved.' I would then take the occasion to underscore with this young man that spiritual maturation comes in the path of having our own spiritual 'powers of discernment trained by constant practice to distinguish good from evil' (Heb. 5:14).

The lesson of this incident just cited is that you and I must be willing to give the appearance of hardheartedness and indifference to perceived need in order that these individuals might see the glory of God in terms of new dimensions in their own spiritual growth. If I had allowed this young man to get to me every time he was convinced he needed my input he would have developed a chronic dependence upon me that would have eaten up hours I should have spent with other people, or in other disciplines and responsibilities of my ministry calculated to benefit the entire congregation. The reason some men are unwilling for this apparent hardheartedness is that they have an unmortified and sometimes wicked desire to keep people nursing at the breasts of their excessive pastoral influence. If that describes you, my brother, I urge you to go to a place called Golgotha and ask God to put that disposition to death. It would be in your best interest to have somebody who loves you and knows you intimately to sit down with you and help you discover why you want people looking to you as the Oracle. We must become like our Lord Jesus Christ as we see Him dealing with the family at Bethany. If we do not seek this dimension of Christlikeness, we will inevitably be faced with ministerial burnout.

THE EXAMPLE OF PAUL

The third biblical example is taken from the life of the apostle Paul.

> On the next day we departed and came to Caesarea, and we entered the house of Philip the evangelist, who was one of the seven, and stayed with him. He had four unmarried daughters, who prophesied. While we were staying for many days, a prophet named Agabus came down from Judea. And coming to us, he took Paul's belt and bound his own feet and hands and said, "Thus says the Holy Spirit, 'This is how the Jews at Jerusalem will bind the man who owns this belt and deliver him into the hands of the Gentiles'" (Acts 21:8-11).

Agabus was given a Spirit-inspired prophecy indicating that when Paul went to Jerusalem he should expect to be apprehended by the Jews. Agabus did not go on to say, 'Therefore, "This is what the Lord says, You shall not go to Jerusalem."' However, the people around Paul who heard this prophecy made an inference from the words of Agabus. Luke records their reaction with these words: 'When we heard this, we and the people there urged him (that is, Paul) not to go up to Jerusalem' (v. 12). In essence they were saying to him, 'We know the will of God for you, Paul. In the light of what is awaiting you in Jerusalem, you must not go there.' 'Then Paul answered, "What are you doing, weeping and breaking my heart? For I am ready not only to be imprisoned but even to die in Jerusalem for the name of the Lord Jesus"' (v. 13). And how did those friends respond to Paul's determination to go to Jerusalem? Did they say among themselves, 'Let the stubborn bullhead receive his due! Let this intransigent, independently-minded man reap the fruit of his independence!'? No, we find them saying, 'Let the will of the Lord be done' (v. 14).

There are times when people individually or collectively will be quite certain they know God's will for you, but you must not let their pressure mislead you. You have pored over the Word of God, particularly those portions which address issues involved in your decision-making concerning the use of your time. Furthermore, you have earnestly sought the face of God in prayer, asking God to give you His promised wisdom. You have sought the counsel of your fellow elders and trusted friends and confidants. By these means you believe you have discovered God's will. Once this discovery of God's will in the outworking of your manifold pastoral responsibilities is made, do not be bullied from a commitment to do it, even by your best friends. To some this may appear as bullheadedness and carnal intransigence. However, it is not bullheadedness with respect to your own independently-informed judgment when your judgment is rooted in earnest prayer, based upon a careful collation of biblical precepts and principles, and is brought through the crucible of the proverbial abundance of counselors (Prov. 11:14; 15:22; 24:6). If we cannot discover God's will in that way, then I have to despair of knowing anything. However, after discovering it, let us not be bullied by the demands of people upon our time or energies.

I say this while admitting there may be the possibility of unusual situations where a brother with strong counsel becomes God's means of persuading to do something other than our previous prayerful and carefully-considered inclination. Who can forget the famous example of the fiery Reformer William Farel prevailing upon John Calvin to remain in Geneva for ministry lest a curse come upon him, though he had only intended to spend the night?[2]

Is there someone reading these pages who is carrying on his back an ugly and irritating monkey of unnecessary guilt? Could it be, my dear brother, that the monkey of guilt has

---

2   Philip Schaff and D.S. Schaff, *History of the Christian Church*, (New York: Charles Schibner's Sons, 1910), VIII.X §81.

been conceived in the womb of allowing people's perceived needs and people's perceived assessment of what you ought to be doing to dictate how you use your time and expend your energies? Rather, a principled structuring of your time and expenditure of your energy should be exercised according to a wise and judicious application of biblical precepts and principles in consultation with wise counselors, and all of this under the canopy of earnest prayer for the promised commodity of divine wisdom (James 1:5). Surely functioning in this way is rendering a measure of real obedience to the command of the Ephesians 5:17 which says, 'Therefore do not be foolish, but understand what the will of the Lord is.'

On the other hand, some of us leave ourselves vulnerable to ministerial burnout by simply taking ourselves too seriously. Periodically I tell myself that if I were to drop dead tomorrow, the world would go on and the work of the Kingdom would not miss a beat. You may not be quite as important as others would lead you to think you are. Part of that monkey on your back may be that you have a wrong assessment of your importance, and therefore you leave yourself vulnerable to pressures arising from a desire to meet others' expectations. Saying no, or not yet, even when it appears we are being insensitive to the needs of people and to the unwritten canons of intimate friendship, may indeed be a very Christlike course of action. Remember the incident of John 11 with Mary, Martha and Lazarus.

This then is the fifth warning against ministerial backsliding and burnout, with particular application to the issue of burnout. *Beware of allowing the use of your time and the proportions of your pastoral labors to be dictated by the perceived needs of your people.*

SEVEN

Beware of Studies Confined to Sermon Preparation

If we would avoid the crippling influence of ministerial burnout, the next warning is of crucial importance. It is this: *Beware of confining your studies to the reading and thinking necessarily and patently precipitated by and connected with your regular sermon preparation.*

Let me explain the wording of this warning. There is an underlying assumption: that you do indeed study, read and think deeply in preparing your sermons. I hope these assumptions are not presumptuous with reference to any man reading these pages. These intellectual and spiritual activities will always be true of us if we take 2 Timothy 2:15 seriously. In this well-known text the apostle commands Timothy to do his utmost to marshal and expend all of his mental and spiritual energies to present himself to God as one approved, that is, a worker who has no legitimate cause for shame before God or man as he cuts a straight course in, or handles aright, the word of truth. There are few things in the experience of a preacher that ought to cause greater shame before God than when he has mishandled the Word of the living God through laziness or carelessness in preparation for preaching. For the true servant of God few things will cause greater shame before men than the discovery on the part of his people that he has inaccurately handled the Word of God because of carelessness or sloppy preparation. Hence this text points Timothy and all who preach and teach the Word of God to engage constantly in that diligent endeavor which is essential to handling aright the word of truth. The application of this command differs from culture to culture and linguistic group to linguistic group. I say these things having close ties with some of our dear brothers in third world situations. I have looked at some of their libraries and have felt both grief and shame considering the paucity of sermon help available to them. But certainly those of us who have any proficiency in the English language have a wealth of material available to us which would, when responsibly used, ensure that we very seldom, if ever, preach an exegetically or theologically inaccurate sermon.

I am assuming that the men reading these pages are committed to serious thinking ordinarily accompanied by wide reading in conjunction with your regular sermon preparation. Of necessity, therefore, much of your reading will be determined by the particular passage or passages that you are expounding in your week by week ministry of the Word of God. Invariably, when I was preaching through the Gospel of Mark, there were 15 commentaries which I consulted with some care before expounding the next paragraph in Mark's Gospel. There were times when the pages read in a particular commentary yielded me absolutely nothing useful, except to confirm the position I had tentatively taken on the passage, since the one taken by that commentator was so bizarre that it confirmed me in my

success in that effort. Unrealistic goals not met become a great barrier to future attempts to make progress in that particular area. Then, in whatever format you map out your plans for your week, put that time on your calendar and guard it as jealously as you would a commitment for a counseling session with one of the distressed sheep in your congregation. Then, choose reading for that time that has no patent or presently-known connection with any preparation of any sermon immediately before you or that you see on the horizon of your preaching responsibilities. Do not allow any whim to take you away from that scheduled time for general reading. Hopefully you will soon be able to block out more time for this discipline.

As pastors our mental growth and health are ordinarily obtained by gradual and modest acquisitions over the long haul, not by large and impressive acquisitions in shorter periods. It is this gradual and modest acquisition that enables us to keep our mental freshness. Exercising our minds in areas other than those directly connected with sermon preparation is like taking a brisk walk in the fresh air. There were many times in past years when after spending the whole morning wrestling with a passage I felt I had hit the wall in terms of a real breakthrough in seeing how to organize and handle the passage homiletically. I would then go out for a midday run in the fresh air. Often while my heartbeat increased and more oxygen was being pumped into my bloodstream, my brain suddenly came alive and the whole sermon or some critical part of the sermon would fall into place. A similar thing often happens in those periods of general reading. You may not even have a remote thought about specific sermon preparation, but your mind, being completely relaxed and focused upon other matters, seems to become unusually fruitful, and the very creative elements which were lacking in your sermon preparation come to life.

VARIETY OF READING

The second recommendation with respect to overcoming the tendencies to mental burnout is a flowering of the first, and it is this: *Seek to establish a pattern of general reading which is both broad and varied, if not always deep and concentrated.* Read everything from systematic theology to Reader's Digest. In this way your mind will not only be grappling with the massive biblical truths of the Word, but you may also encounter a few humorous incidents that will make you laugh. Sometimes a laugh in the middle of the day is the best tonic for a weary mind. I am so thankful that for many years I had a study that overlooked a large back yard (a 'garden' for my British readers). In that yard I was able to see fat groundhogs waddling to their holes at the fringe of the yard, rabbits hopping about, squirrels whose antics at times precipitated irrepressible laughter, and at times even deer, along with many species of birds. Believe it or not, one winter a red fox would snuggle up to a fence which constituted the boundary of our yard and sun himself in the late afternoon. I found many times that just concentrating on the wildlife in my backyard for a few minutes enabled my mind to regain its resilience. In the same way, it may be in reading a book of church history or a biography that you will come across an incident that will greatly refresh your spirit, or call you into fresh commitment to the Lord, or drive you to your knees giving you fresh confirmation of a specific truth. Seek to read everything from Professor John Murray to *The Pilgrim's Progress.* Read periodicals that keep you in touch with what is going on in your own generation. Seek to establish a reading program that over the course of six months is taking you over a wide range of theology, history, pastoral concerns, polemics, current issues, etc.[1]

A PERIOD OF INTENSIVE READING

Thirdly, as part of the remedy for mental burnout, I would like to suggest that *you attempt to secure at least one lengthy period of intense and extensive reading each year.* I would not suggest that

---

1   See my *Pastoral Theology* DVD series, Module 2, Lecture 6; also audio cassette # MI-MB-16, available from The Trinity Pulpit of Trinity Baptist Church, Montville, New Jersey.

you plan to do this on your annual vacation, especially if your children are still under your roof. If you turn your vacation into a study break you are liable to elicit more than frowns from your wife and your children, and rightly so. To do this would also mean robbing yourself of the emotional, mental and psychological refreshment which ought to be some of the major benefits secured by a proper vacation.

Assuming you have some deep ties of intimate friendship with some ministers of like mind and heart, I suggest the following scenario. First of all, set aside some time to sit down with the men in your congregation to whom you have a more formal accountability like your fellow elders and deacons and who, with you, plan the preaching schedule in your assembly. Seek to persuade them to read and discuss with you this section of this book, or to listen to my pastoral theology lectures on the benefits of general reading in the life of the man of God. Then, seek to convince them that if they want you to be the best preacher you can possibly be, one who gives them the fruit of an active mind not afflicted with mental burnout, that it would be in their best interest for you to have at least one uninterrupted two-week period each year when you schedule a pulpit exchange with a known and trusted fellow minister. Then, during those two weeks, all of the time that you would normally take for sermon preparation will be used for concentrated, in-depth reading in a specific area. On the Saturday afternoons and evenings of those two weeks you could then take some sermons that you have preached to your people, carefully study them, pray them afresh into your heart, pray for the Spirit's blessing upon them, and preach them to your minister-friend's congregation. You would then have a two-week period when the hours normally spent in regular sermon preparation would be spent in this kind of intense, extensive, general reading in an area of particular interest.

Such a plan could, under the blessing of God, result in a new measure of mental alertness, general knowledge or specific knowledge in a given area that would become a lifetime companion. For example, suppose you made it your goal that in the two-week period you were going to go through large sections of Richard Baxter's *Directory*.[2] Identifying specific aspects of pastoral concerns you have faced, you might go through the index of the *Directory*, picking out those sections which address those specific areas of concern. You would then give yourself to serious reading of those particular sections. You would come away from those two weeks a much more adequately-equipped pastor to engage in the areas of biblical casuistry so vital to a Bible-based counseling ministry. Furthermore, you would have made an acquaintance with Baxter that will enable you in the future to refer your people to specific sections in the *Directory* that might be helpful to them.

Or another suggestion is that you take one or two volumes of John Owen, or select portions of some of the volumes of Owen that you have yearned to read, but never felt you had the time required to do so. While you may have read some in Volume 6 and received great profit from that, there is so much rich material in the other volumes, particularly volumes 1, 2, 3 and 7. In blocking out that time for concentrated reading and arranging for the pulpit exchange with your ministerial friend you will make a very solemn commitment that the hours normally spent in sermon preparation will indeed be spent in that kind of focused reading. In giving yourself to such a concentrated exposure to a great and godly mind you will profit intellectually. No one with any degree of intellectual and spiritual sensitivity can come into close and concentrated contact with a large soul and a keen mind and not absorb some of the impress of that greatness upon his own mind and spirit. This kind of reading engaged in with conscious dependence upon the Holy Spirit will bring benefits that we cannot measure. Our people may well come to us after such

---

2   *The Practical Works of Richard Baxter, Vol. 1: A Christian Directory*, published by Soli Deo Gloria ministries. This is a voluminous treatise of Puritan casuistry, offering specific pastoral counsel and guidance in many practical areas of Christian living.

a reading Sabbatical and say to us, 'You know, Pastor, ever since that pulpit exchange and that two-week reading time, there has been a freshness in your preaching. There has been an element of refreshing imagery and precision of statement that was not there before. Are you consciously doing something different?' What has happened? You have lived for two weeks with a man who had the unique ability to state things with Spirit-imparted wisdom, precision and profound depth of insight. Without being consciously aware of the fact your mind has absorbed some of those qualities and they are now finding expression in your preaching to the enrichment of your people and to the increased usefulness of your own pulpit endeavors. Your experience would be a validation of the words of Solomon: 'Whoever walks with the wise becomes wise' (Prov. 13:20).

Let me offer a final suggestion along these lines. It may be that you have never worked through John Calvin's classic *Institutes of the Christian Religion*. You would receive long-term benefit if you determine that in that first two-week reading period, you would start at Book 1, Section 1, and begin a disciplined, systematic reading of the entire work. It most likely will take you several such reading Sabbaticals to complete the endeavor. However, what you will accomplish is to make the *Institutes* a right-hand companion for your sermon preparation and your other pastoral labors for the rest of your life and your ministerial labors. No doubt there will also be other sections in the *Institutes* to which you will turn for devotional purposes as well. Having exposed your mind to the master of Geneva, there will be many occasions when various aspects of sermon preparation and pastoral labors will trigger an association in your mind which will cause you to return to the *Institutes* for help and direction.

By means of that concentrated reading period you have brought alongside you someone who has sat on one of your bookshelves for years benignly smiling at you when you pass by him, while to you he is mute. He has never spoken to you in connection with your sermon preparation. He has never spoken to you concerning matters of pastoral casuistry and then drawn alongside you in a thorny pastoral counseling situation. Now he sits there on one of your bookshelves, but he is silent no longer. He is ready to talk to you for the rest of your life because you gave him two weeks, or possibly four or six weeks, to let him talk to you for a considerable number of hours.

If you make one such acquisition each year, what would happen in twenty years? We must think in terms of this gradual and steady acquisition over the long haul. I do not think that such an arrangement as I have suggested is unreasonable or unattainable. I wish someone had counseled me along these lines early in my ministry. However, I am thankful that for twenty years it was my privilege to lecture on pastoral theology in the Trinity Ministerial Academy. The initial preparation and constant revision of those lectures kept me reading widely in many areas other than the reading directly connected with my weekly sermon preparation.

The necessity for a mental Sabbath

My fourth suggestion as remedy for and preventive of mental burnout is this: *Attempt to secure a weekly mental Sabbath for the refreshment of your intellectual faculties.* Why do some men experience recurring patterns of intellectual burnout? It is because they have no intellectual and mental Sabbath. As a preacher your mind is being driven to its most intense activities with the approach of each Lord's Day. Then, on the Lord's Day, the delivery of that which you have prepared raises your mental exertions to an even higher level. Then, if you do not give your mental faculties a Sabbath, but immediately place them into harness on Monday morning and whip them throughout the week until the next Lord's Day, you are very likely setting yourself up for some form of mental burnout. Your mental faculties may cry out 'Master, please give me a little rest.' You have indeed become a cruel master to your mind. You do not listen to its reasonable and earnest plea for rest. As a result, when you sit down later in the week to do the spadework of careful exegesis, you find that you have little heart for it. Finally, the tired old mule of your overstretched mind simply rolls over on its side, looks up at you and says, 'Shoot me if you will, but I am going nowhere. The whip in your hand no longer intimidates me.' What has happened? You have made inordinate demands upon your intellectual and mental faculties and now it has caught up with you in the form of mental burnout.

The older writers on pastoral theology were dogmatic as they addressed this very issue. Thomas Murphy, a Presbyterian minister of another generation, in his book entitled *Pastoral Theology*, wrote concerning the study habits of the preacher:

> We have said that this daily routine we propose is only for five days in the week. On the Sabbath the minister should have nothing to do with any other mental efforts than those of his public exercises. All preparations should be fully made before the Lord's Day arrives. On every account the slovenly habits of finishing sermons on the sacred day should be most strenuously *avoided. We would also earnestly recommend that Monday be observed as a day of mental and bodily rest. The minister must have his resting day as well as other men or he will suffer the consequences.* His physical constitution demands it. If it is denied, in time he will break down in health, as hundreds are doing. Nor must it be supposed that devoting one day of the week to absolute rest will be a loss of time in the end. No; the work of the other days will be more vigorous, the physical and *mental tone* will be kept up, and at the end of the year far more will be accomplished. One day of wakeful, energetic work is worth three or four spent in half dreaming and forcing oneself to unattractive tasks (emphases mine).[3]

It seems to me that Dr. Murphy has visited you and me in some of our 'burnout' seasons, has he not? And he is right. Over

---

3   *The Practical Works of Richard Baxter, Vol. 1*, p. 104.

the course of many years in preparing my lectures in pastoral theology, I have had the privilege of discovering and reading many of these older writers. Almost without exception they give advice similar to this we have cited. They urge upon the preacher the necessity of a mental Sabbath. If in the multitude of counselors there is safety, then the counsel of these seasoned pastor-preacher-theologians should carry immense weight with us. These were men who made their mark as preachers and also as working pastors. Then, toward the end of their days they looked back over their shoulders and said to their younger brethren coming behind them, 'Young men, this is the course of sustained usefulness.'

My preacher brother, your sanctified, elastic and fully active mind is the grand workshop for your sermonizing. If it becomes overstretched and dull through mental burnout, if it becomes void of fresh raw materials through limited acquisitions, or worn out because it is given no rest or refreshment, then your people will suffer. You will feel ashamed. You will feel legitimate guilt that you have placed yourself in the pathway not only to ministerial burnout, but also to ministerial backsliding. Therefore, my counsel to you is to avoid the burnout that may well be fueled *by limiting your reading to that done in conjunction with specific sermon preparation.*

Eight

Beware of Hiding Your Real Humanity

My seventh warning is one which addresses a constant temptation for men who are set apart to 'labor in the word and in doctrine'. It is a warning of particular relevance to those whose full-time work is the ministry. While it may also be a temptation to pastors who support themselves by other means of employment, the level of temptation is nowhere near as great for them. The warning is this: *Beware of allowing your official position and functions in the ministry to become a wall behind which to hide your real humanity, or a cocoon within which to imprison your humanity.*

Let me explain the ideas wrapped up in this warning. The Scriptures inform us that even the apostles and their companions acknowledged that the treasure of their Gospel stewardship was contained in 'jars of clay' (2 Cor. 4:7). Such a metaphor is not at all flattering, but that is precisely what we are. Clay jars contain this Gospel treasure, Paul continues to explain, 'to show that the surpassing power belongs to God and not to us.'

Now we must ask, 'What precisely is that clay jar?' It is nothing other than our frail humanity, our imperfectly-sanctified humanity, our not-yet-glorified humanity, both with respect to our spirits and to our bodies. However, when we begin to take seriously the high biblical standard for an overseer, both with regard to his character and to his work, the devil can use our very sensitivity to that standard to nudge us into creating a wall behind which we attempt to hide our frail humanity, or to fashion a cocoon within which we seek to imprison it. For example, when we take seriously the standard of 1 Timothy 3:2 and Titus 1:6 which requires blamelessness, and then add to that such imperatives as are found in 1 Timothy 4:12 and Titus 2:7, we begin to fear that if we are transparent and honest before our people we will lose our grip upon their consciences in the light of the things we know about ourselves that clearly manifest our clay-jar constitution.

We mistakenly think allowing any clear and natural expressions of felt weakness, crippling fears, discouragements and struggles with our own sins will erode people's confidence in us. We fear that transparency in such matters will lower the biblical standard for the ministry, and then we begin to make the ministry itself a wall behind which to hide our frail and imperfectly-sanctified humanity. Or worse yet, we make of the ministry a cocoon to imprison that imperfect humanity, not allowing it to find proper biblical expressions. This building up of internal current, this unnatural damming up and closing in of our humanity, often leads to ministerial burnout and breakdown.

If we are true men of God we passionately desire to be models of the grace of God and the power of the Gospel, of self-control and manly courage. We mistakenly think, therefore, that we cannot indulge in the innocent and honest expressions of the human emotions associated with the experience of grief, of intense and ecstatic joy, of disappointment, of fear, of shortcomings and of failure. Certainly not publicly! Oh yes, they reason, it may be acceptable to express these things to one's wife or older children or to an intimate confidant or friend. However, others go even further and construct this wall and fabricate this cocoon so that they do not express these elements of their 'clayness' even to their most intimate companions and friends.

What is the result? It is this. Any attack upon our *humanity* does not have its origin in the revealed will of God and is essentially self-destructive. God's grace in Christ and God the Holy Spirit wage an all-out warfare against sin. But they *never war against our humanity*, even as that humanity presently exists in a fallen world with the 'not yet' experience of saving grace. Any effort to hide that humanity behind the wall or to imprison it in the cocoon will result in an unhealthy and plastic unnaturalness. Eventually our real humanity will find outlets of expression that are neither godly nor healthy.

Here is another way to express my concern. If wearing your clerical collar makes you a fundamentally different human being from what you are without it something is drastically wrong. Somehow you have allowed your ministerial office and function to become a wall for hiding your humanity or a cocoon for imprisoning it. Mere clothing should not make you a fundamentally different man. Your divine call to the Christian ministry is not a summons to de-humanize yourself.

REJECTING A DEFECTIVE THEOLOGY

What, then, is the remedy for this evil? First, you must recognize and reject what may well be a defective theology of the purposes and dynamics of redemptive grace and bring your working theology of the Christian life into line with the Word of God. I would stress this: redemptive grace has a controversy only with sin, not with humanity. God's word to Joseph was 'you shall call his name Jesus, for he will save his people from their sins' (Matt. 1:21). He has come to save us from our sins, but not from our humanity. The Scriptures clearly affirm that the culmination of redemptive grace is the resurrection of the body, and not merely the perfection of the spirit or soul after death. Though it will be wonderful to 'be away from the body and at home with the Lord' (2 Cor. 5:8), the apex of redemptive grace will be our resurrection day. We will then once more be fully human as God intended human existence. Meanwhile, we that are in this tabernacle do 'groan, longing to put on our heavenly dwelling' (2 Cor. 5:1-2). Paul also teaches that the sons of God long for the full manifestation of their sonship, even the redemption of our bodies (Rom. 8:23). Whatever is essentially human about us, redemptive grace increasingly liberates from the effects of sin and enhances it with the graces of the Holy Spirit, but it does not pummel it, let alone suppress, distort or seek to obliterate it. Again I say, grace does not wage war with what is essentially human, but only with that which is sinful.

It is for this very reason that Paul declares in 1 Timothy 4:1-5 that regarding merely human pleasures as sinful is done under demonic influences. Apparently some were teaching that the pleasures of the sexual union in marriage and the pure sensuous delights experienced in eating all kinds of food were antithetical to the highest expressions of piety and advancement in spiritual stature. The purveyors of this teaching regarded these things as too carnal, human and earthly. They were forbidding people to marry, assuming that married couples would frequently engage in and enjoy the sexual union, and to salivate over a juicy steak, and to smile with pleasure while they were eating it. The apostle says that it is demons who instigate such teaching! The demons who control pagan philosophical and religious thought were causing men to teach that earthly human pleasures were essentially evil. However, Paul makes it clear that the God of grace is not at war with what is essentially human and good in His creation, but only with that which is sinful.

Understanding this truth will liberate us with respect to how our calling and function in the ministry should relate to the natural and full expressions of what we are in our created humanity. We will feel no compulsion to be under this unnatural strain: 'I have my dog collar on, and I cannot be an ordinary man. I cannot speak like an ordinary man, but I must have a special ministerial tone in my voice, especially when I pray in public. I can't laugh from my belly and from my toes when I watch monkeys play with one another at the local zoo.' The cleric laughing his head off at monkeys? Shameful! My brother, I believe God laughed at the cavorting of monkeys in the Garden of Eden. I believe he still chuckles at them when they continue their cavorting in the depths of those jungles where no human eye can see them.

God never called a man to the Gospel ministry with a view to dehumanizing him. If you have a defective theology of the purposes and dynamics of redemptive grace, and if you impose it upon yourself with respect to how you conduct yourself among your people, both in public and in private, you will inevitably be creating both a wall for hiding and a cocoon for imprisoning. This will make you a prime candidate for ministerial breakdown and burnout. The only answer to this aberration and its dangers is to align your theology of the purposes and dynamics of redemptive grace with the Word of God, and consciously to reject any demonic suggestions that would drive you to any kind of asceticism, whether physical or emotional and psychological.

THE EXAMPLE OF JESUS
Second, if you would avoid both the wall and the cocoon, I urge you to get your examples of sanctified ministerial humanity from the Word of God, especially from the example of our Lord Jesus Christ and of the apostle Paul. With respect to this principle, three texts ought to be our constant companions. The first is Romans 8:29. Here we are told that 'whom he foreknew he also predestined to be conformed to the image of his Son.' The second

text is 2 Corinthians 3:18 which reads, 'And we all, with unveiled face, beholding the glory of the Lord, are being transformed into the same image from one degree of glory to another. For this comes from the Lord who is the Spirit.' The third text is 1 John 2:6 which says, 'whoever says he abides in him ought to walk in the same way in which he walked.' The common denominator of these three texts is obviously the fact that conformity to Christ is the central concern of the purpose of God in redemptive grace. This being so, it is incumbent upon us constantly to be studying the life of our Lord Jesus Christ recorded in the Scriptures, constantly praying that the Spirit of God may do His work of progressively conforming us to that image of our Blessed Lord. In our Lord Jesus Christ we behold sinless, spotless, perfect, but real humanity – humanity as God intended, and as the new humanity will be in the consummation of redemption. Then Christ will be the Elder Brother of that vast host of His redeemed family, all perfectly reflecting His image. Because God's controversy with sin in us is indeed being manifested in our progressive sanctification, we will necessarily become increasingly like our Savior, not only in His moral perfections, but in His unvarnished, transparent, and pure humanity.

Let me heartily recommend reading periodically B. B. Warfield's masterful treatise on 'The Emotional Life of Our Lord'.[1] Warfield underscores the fact that in our Lord Jesus, the only perfect man since the fall of our first parents, we are beholding sinless humanity, especially in the manifestation of sinless human emotions. The Gospels reveal our Lord living and breathing, walking and speaking, ministering and interacting with real people in the same context in which we are called upon to live and to minister. However, it is evident that with our Lord Jesus Christ there was no hiding of His pure humanity behind a wall of artificial ministerial stiffness, nor was there any

---

1   B. B. Warfield, "The Emotional Life of Our Lord", first published in 1912, is reprinted in *The Person and Work of Christ*, (ed. S.G. Craig; Philadelphia: P&R, 1950), pp. 93 ff.

effort to imprison that sinless humanity in anything remotely approaching a 'clerical cocoon'.

For example, when He came to the temple and saw all that evil men had done to His Father's house of prayer, He became angry with a righteous and holy anger. He did not allow that anger to become a pent-up and unexpressed emotion, saying to Himself, 'No holy teacher can be manifestly angry. Put on a stoical face and go into the temple and occasionally nudge a table or two, tweak an ox on his flanks, and graciously request that the money changers leave as soon as possible.' No! Both John's Gospel which records the initial temple cleansing and the Synoptics which record the later cleansing portray graphically a man whose soul was full of fury, a fury which extended to His fingertips when with a scourge He drove out all the money changers, the beasts, and overturned the tables and all that was on them. All of His actions belonged to a man on a mission. It was evident that in every cell of His being zeal for His Father's house was consuming Him. However, in all of this passionate emotion He yet remained 'holy, innocent, unstained', and 'separated from sinners' (Heb. 7:26).

Mark 3 reports an attempt of the Pharisees to catch our Lord in a compromising Sabbath activity. In that setting Mark informs us that Jesus 'looked around at them with anger, grieved at their hardness of heart' (v. 5), and He proceeded to heal the man with the withered hand. Our Lord's grief at the hardness of the Pharisees' hearts merged into a righteous anger that obviously found its way into the very look on His countenance. There was perfect consistency in every facet of His holy humanity. He did not repress either the grief now merged into anger, or the manifestation of that anger in His countenance. The very one who spoke of Himself by saying, 'I am gentle and lowly in heart' (Matt. 11:29), is the one who in this incident recorded by Mark did not hide the expressions of sanctified human anger behind a wall of false ministerial restraint or contain such expressions of emotion in a self-made cocoon of unwarranted and unrighteous reserve.

Luke records the incident of our Lord's visit to the home of a Pharisee (Luke 7:36-50). Our Lord was denied several common courtesies typically afforded any ordinary guest in such a home. He not only took note of this fact, but He mildly reproved His host for this social oversight (v. 44). Was it sinful for our Lord to take note of the oversight and then to speak about it to His host? Should our Lord have exercised that love which 'covers a multitude of sins'? Had our Lord's reaction been tinged with the slightest taint of sinfulness, He would not be our sinless Savior. No, in His pure and unsullied humanity our Lord felt the sting of the social omissions, and He did not hide that fact behind a wall of plastic ministerial composure or seek to contain that insult in a self-made ministerial cocoon constructed of neutered human emotions.

Examples of this kind could be multiplied from the Gospel records. Jesus clearly expressed His disappointment over the unbelief and slowness of heart manifested by His disciples. He openly and unashamedly wailed over Jerusalem as He entered it for the last time. Furthermore, Matthew and Luke record that there was a period in His life, identified by the words 'at that time' (Matt. 11:25) and 'in that same hour' (Luke 10:21), when our Lord rejoiced greatly in His spirit and expressed that rejoicing in an exuberant prayer of thanksgiving to His heavenly Father for His absolute sovereignty in the revealing and the hiding of Himself from men. Standing by the tomb of Lazarus, He faced the horrible reality of death and unashamedly and openly wept (John 11:35). In that same setting, experiencing such a revulsion in the presence of death, and knowing that He was death's ultimate and final conqueror, He does something which John describes with a verb that one would use to describe the snorting and ground-pawing activities of a warhorse (John 11:38).

The disarming transparency of our Lord Jesus was perhaps nowhere more evident than when He obviously allowed His disciples to hear Him when He was praying to His heavenly Father. The Gospels record several incidents in which our Lord poured out His holy soul into the ears of His Father. Although the clay of His real humanity was not at all mixed with sin as it is in us, surely the prayer in Gethsemane reveals that our Lord was totally free from making any attempt to hide His true human wrestlings behind a ministerial wall or to bury them in a carnally-constructed cocoon. He made it plain as He went into Gethsemane that He keenly felt the need for the companionship of His disciples when He asked them to watch with Him. Then, while within sight of the disciples, the crushing burden of the cup of His impending sufferings drove Him to the ground again and again in a paroxysm of intense agony. The favored three disciples stayed close enough to Him that they could hear the agonizing cry, thrice repeated: 'not my will, but yours, be done' (Matt. 26:44). When our Lord returned from the short distance by which He had separated Himself from the three disciples He found them asleep. His holy soul was deeply disappointed. He did not hide the 'clay' of that disappointment. Rather, He said to them, no doubt in words tinged with an obvious expression of disappointment, 'So, could you not watch with me one hour?' (Matt. 26:40).

Surely it is not going beyond the clear testimony of Scripture to assert that our Lord Jesus Christ is indeed the perfect example of ministerial transparency and of the unashamed revealing of one's humanity: holy anger, bitter disappointment, ecstatic joy, brokenness of heart, holy frustration and openly-acknowledged need for human companionship. All these things were true of our Lord and are taken from the clear testimony of the Word of God. There is no indication whatsoever that our Lord believed He could only accomplish His sacred mission by erecting a wall of excessive ministerial reserve and by creating a cocoon within which He would imprison those expressions of His true humanity.

THE EXAMPLE OF THE APOSTLE PAUL
Consider also the example of the apostle Paul. On several occasions he urged his readers to be imitators of him, even

as he was of Christ (e.g., 1 Cor. 4:16; 11:1; Phil. 3:17). As we survey the book of Acts and the letters which that great man of God wrote, we find a man who knew nothing of the ministerial 'wall' and the clerical 'cocoon'. For example, he was utterly transparent and agonizingly honest concerning the fact that he lived with the continuous agitation and frustration of two contrary principles in constant warfare within his breast. Romans 7:14-25 is the legacy of his honesty.[2] He lays out the painful reality of that warfare for all generations to see. While that passage reflects only one dimension of the Christian life, it is a real dimension of that life.

Further, in other places Paul unashamedly acknowledges that he experienced periods of intense loneliness and longing for human companionship. In his second letter to the Corinthians he writes: 'But God, who comforts the downcast [depressed], comforted us by the coming of Titus' (2 Cor. 7:6). Here is this giant of a man informing us that he had periods of being cast down or depressed, and that God's remedy for that depression on one occasion was not a fresh infilling of the Holy Spirit, but the visit of a beloved brother and fellow laborer in Christ. How crassly human!

Do these frank acknowledgments of the fact that Paul had the treasure in a clay jar cause us to respect him less? No; just the opposite is true. It causes us to love and admire him the more for writing in ways consistent with the biblical teaching that God's grace wars not with nature, but only with sin. The man who wrote the words, 'we have this treasure in jars of clay', (2 Cor. 4:7) was not afraid to let his clay show.

Many years ago it was my privilege to minister in a one-day pastors' conference in the Midwest. One of the other speakers was a retired US Army chaplain, and during the lunch hour he and I sat together. In the course of our lunchtime conversation

2   I am aware of the controversy over the meaning of this passage. However, I believe the basic position taken by John Murray, Sinclair Ferguson, J. I. Packer and other commentators both old and new is correct, and that the newer position taken by Douglas Moo and others is wanting.

this retired chaplain, considerably older than I, asked me a question that seemed rather strange at the time: 'Do you believe the Scripture which says "we have this treasure in jars of clay?"' With respect for his age and military background, I answered him, 'Yes sir, I do.' He then responded with words that have been my delightful and liberating companion for several decades. While I could not say under oath that these were the exact words he spoke, the gist of them was unforgettable. He said to me, 'Young man, if it is true that we have the treasure in jars of clay, don't be afraid to let the clay show. The treasure is never more precious than when the clay is showing.' Those words have urged me again and again to a life of ministerial transparency and the vulnerability that comes when we refuse to allow our ministerial position and functions to morph into an ugly wall behind which we attempt to hide our humanity or into a grotesque cocoon within which we seek to imprison that humanity.

My dear fellow minister, the remedy for all this wall-making and cocoon-construction is not only to get straight our theology of the purposes and dynamics of redemptive grace, but it is to get our examples of sanctified ministerial humanity from the Word of God, particularly as we study the life of our Lord Jesus Christ and that of the apostle Paul.

I fully acknowledge that the sanctified expressions of our true humanity will flow along the channels determined in great measure by our native temperament. In addition to this fact, they will also be disciplined by the pressure of Spirit-imparted love to respect the legitimate cultural mores of the situations in which we live and minister. Also, we will seek to restrain ourselves from expressions of our humanity that would be perceived as unseemly. Since love is not 'rude' (1 Cor. 13:5), we will not indulge in things that are boorish, coarse and unnecessarily offensive under the guise that we are just 'expressing our humanity'. Such things would indeed be an expression of our humanity, but of our sinful humanity. Yet the peculiar channels of our native temperament and the sanctified restraints of love have no affinity with the wall or the cocoon. If you live with the walls or the cocoon you are denying a fundamental truth of the Gospel, that truth declared by our Lord when He said anyone whom the Son sets free is 'free indeed' (John 8:36). By the grace and power of our Lord Jesus Christ, mediated to us through the Gospel, we are not only freed from the guilt and dominion of sin, but we are set free to become fully human beings. Perhaps, my brother, you are placing yourself under that oppressive yoke of seeking to be something other than a fully human person. Such a yoke is never an easy yoke, and such a burden is never light. Straining to live under this yoke may well be the reason some of my readers are in a state of ministerial burnout.

Another tragic result of the wall and the cocoon is that you place an insuperable barrier between yourself and the ordinary mortals to whom you minister. Your people do not see you as a fellow mortal who struggles when and where they struggle, who weeps when and where they weep, who grieves when and where they grieve, and shouts for joy when and where they shout. Are you really comfortable with a ministry that has little rapport with and meager measures of expressed affinity for imperfectly sanctified but real humanity? If you are satisfied with such a ministry, and if you believe you can give a good account of such a ministry when you stand before your Savior at the Last Day, then you may continue to hide your real humanity behind your clerical wall and shut it up in your clerical cocoon. Your people may stand in awe of you from a distance and for a while admire you. However, they will not open their hearts to you and expose their deepest struggles and troubles, or their highest joys and their most disturbing questions, because you seem to be a creature totally different from themselves.

Why is it that we feel we can come and pour out our hearts to our heavenly Father with unfettered and unembarrassed liberty? According to the writer to the Hebrews it is precisely because we know and are confident that 'we have not an high priest which cannot be touched with the feeling of our infirmities; but was in all points tempted like as we are, yet without sin' (4:15, KJV). On the basis of what we read in the Scriptures concerning our Lord Jesus Christ, living, laboring, relating and ministering in this broken and fallen world with no 'wall' behind which He attempted to hide His real humanity and no 'cocoon' within which He sought to imprison that humanity, we therefore feel free 'with confidence' to 'draw near to the throne of grace' (Heb. 4:15-16, ESV). The Holy Spirit through the Word of God continually endears our Savior to us as we behold His glory. No little part of that glory is the radiance of His spotlessly pure but absolutely transparent, vulnerable, accessible and endearing humanity. We see Him as truly one of our kind, sin only excepted.

My brother, if you would have men, women, boys and girls across a broad spectrum of backgrounds and personalities, with a broad spectrum of sins, trials, perplexities and questions coming to you, feeling free to pour out their hearts in an honest acknowledgment of their condition, then you must be a patently human being, one of their kind. In other words, you must become more and more like your truly human Savior. Yes, He was and is essential, undiminished and undiluted Deity. Yet 'the Word became flesh and dwelt among us' (John 1:14). That flesh which He took to Himself was likewise essential, undiminished and undiluted humanity. Sin is not an essential part of humanity. It is a grotesque intrusion. It is that vile moral intrusion with which the grace and power of the Gospel are in conflict. With what is essentially human, grace and the Gospel have no controversy. Rather, redemptive provisions and power are operative to liberate that humanity and to conform it more and more to the likeness of our Elder Brother. Again, remember that 'whoever says he abides in him ought to walk in the same way in which he walked' (1 John 2:6).

May God be pleased to rivet this seventh warning to your conscience: *Beware of allowing your official position and functions in the ministry to become a wall behind which to hide your real humanity, or a cocoon within which to imprison your humanity.*

Closing prayer

Our Father, we are so thankful that we need not be ashamed of our humanity. We are deeply ashamed of our sins. We would grieve and mourn afresh over what we are because of our original union with Adam, and what we were from the moment of our conception, and what we continue to be in the light of our indwelling sin. We would not treat lightly these things that are so offensive to You. Help us to appreciate, not only what we are in Christ, but all that You have made us and all that Your grace and power are doing to restore us to the original image in which we were made, grace that will one day bring us into perfect conformity to Your beloved Son.

Teach us how to be exemplary ministers of the Gospel without any unnatural walls or cocoons that would hide or suppress our sanctified humanity in all of its legitimate expressions. Help us in these things so that many of Your servants will be wonderfully preserved from the backsliding and burnout that have slain thousands and crippled multitudes. Be pleased as well to rescue some who are presently in the state of burnout because of the walls and the cocoon. We plead for these mercies, believing that Your giving them would glorify You. We lay our praises and our petitions before You through Jesus Christ our Lord. Amen.

WARNINGS

AGAINST

CREDIBILITY WASHOUT

NINE

Beware of Ministry with Neglect
of Your Physical Body

I am fully aware of the fact that the concerns related
to ministerial backsliding and burnout overlap and
interpenetrate one another at many points. However,
generally speaking I have regarded ministerial *backsliding* as
that state into which we enter by neglecting the fundamental
spiritual disciplines ordained by God for our *spiritual* well-
being. Ministerial *burnout* ordinarily occurs as a result of
neglecting the fundamental *mental and physical* disciplines
ordained by God for our *general* well-being. In the former we
are dealing with issues related primarily to *sin* with antidotes
rooted in the Scriptures. In the latter we are dealing with issues
related primarily to *nature* with antidotes rooted primarily in
general revelation. Understanding this twofold distinction is
critical. As we come to the eighth warning concerning these

two plagues, this distinction between them will become even clearer. The eighth warning is this: *Beware of seeking to serve God in the office and functions of the ministry as though you were a disembodied spirit, rather than a creature of flesh and blood.*

Again, I will follow the basic outline I have used all along in opening up these various warnings. I will explain the significance of the words of the warning, and then give the biblical antidote to that particular danger.

In the ordinary course of their ministries many men experience what appears to them to be the tell-tale signs of backsliding. Prolonged dullness in prayer and the lack of mental and spiritual delight and profit from personal Bible reading greatly trouble them. Over the course of many years I have had numerous men sit in my study, call me or write to me, expressing their concern about such matters. In most cases they have already concluded that their problem must be fundamentally a spiritual one.

However, after close examination of the patterns of their lives, on a number of occasions it has become quite evident to me that the fundamental cause for what seemed to be a condition of spiritual declension was, in reality, something entirely different. They were not guilty of those things which ordinarily precipitate spiritual declension, whether sins of commission or of omission. Rather, they were guilty of neglect of those means ordained by God for emotional, mental and physical resilience. The neglect of those means was now taking its toll upon the totality of their lives, including their ability to benefit from the spiritual disciplines by which they have generally nourished their own souls.

Others have complained of a lack of mental vigor at the desk and of chronic weariness in fulfilling their basic ministerial tasks. Still others have complained to me that they have entered an Elijah-like depressed state in which, though they were not contemplating suicide, they have almost wished that God would do the job for them.

When men in this condition have sought my counsel they have often done so expecting that I would go after the sins of unbelief, a lack of zeal for the glory of God and the advancement of His kingdom, or that I would engage in some form of spiritual probing seeking to uncover some secret sin in their lives. If such things were indeed the cause of their condition, they were opening their hearts to me because they were willing to identify those issues and to deal with them in a biblical way. However, as a result of asking some very basic questions concerning their patterns of diet, exercise, rest, conscientious observance of a day off and a simple thing such as the amount of their caffeine consumption, it has often become clear to me that their problems did not necessarily have their roots in basic spiritual issues, except for the spiritual implications of this problem I am about to identify. The real cause for their condition lay in their failure to recognize that they were men of flesh and blood. For all intents and purposes, they were seeking to serve God and their people as though they were disembodied spirits like the angels.

Angels have nothing to do but to give thought to performing the will of God with spontaneous and joyful alacrity. They never give one thought to sleep, nutrition or physical exercise. They surround the throne of God waiting for the first intimations of God's will for them. Upon the disclosure of that will, they go forth to do service to the heirs of salvation with unwearied vigor and undiminished energy. No angel ever returned from his latest assigned task and approached God's throne to receive his next assignment with his eyes drooping from weariness, out of breath and in desperate need of a midday siesta. Angels have no problems of this kind in the service which they render to God because they render that service as disembodied spirits. Yes, they are occasionally given by God a temporary physical subsistence when the nature of a specific form of their service demands it. However, our service to God must be rendered to Him in our flesh and blood existence, with all the limitations and necessities that such an existence entails. Additional burdens are placed upon our service rendered to God in our bodily existence because our bodies are affected with the results of sin.

When a man of God who is serious about his calling functions as if he were, in fact, an angel-like disembodied spirit, sooner or later he will experience things that to him may appear as the symptoms of backsliding. In reality, they are often the signs of ministerial burnout. If a man is ignorant of and indifferent to such matters as wholesome eating habits, adequate patterns of sleep, a healthy weight status and the place and benefits of regular exercise and recreation, such a man is being set up for an extreme case of ministerial burnout. Hence my warning that we must beware of seeking to serve God in the office and functions of the ministry as if we were disembodied spirits rather than men of flesh and blood, even sin-afflicted flesh and blood.

Having explained the words of the warning, I will now address the cure and the preventive to this cause of ministerial burnout. The antidote is comprised of five strands of exhortation. If these exhortations are made matters of conscientious practice, they could become with God's blessing the means of both preventing and rescuing many preachers from ministerial burnout. The first four exhortations are ones with which I would attempt to bind the conscience of every reader. In the fifth, I will only try to influence your judgment by what I believe is the wise counsel of some men from the past. However, with the first four I am not at all ashamed to say that I am attempting to bind your conscience, since these first four exhortations are comprised of explicitly revealed biblical duties.

Also, I am conscious in addressing this area of concern that I will be moving beyond just the issues of ministerial burnout. In reality, I will be moving into the area of 'credibility washout', a condition in which there has been a tragic and massive erosion of our credibility as examples to the flock.

THE SIXTH COMMANDMENT

The first of these five strands of exhortation is this: *Remember your obligation to render evangelical obedience to the sixth commandment.*

I trust that the readers of these pages are persuaded that when God applies His salvation to sinners He always implants in those sinners a conscious desire to render evangelical obedience to His law (Ezek. 36:26-27). 'Evangelical obedience' defines that kind of obedience which flows from the power and the motives present in the heart and life of everyone who has been regenerated and has truly embraced God's salvation as offered in the Gospel of our Lord and Savior Jesus Christ. The work of Christ for us has utterly, radically and permanently changed our relationship to the condemning power of the law (Gal. 3:13; Rom. 8:3). The work of the Holy Spirit in us has utterly, radically and permanently changed our disposition to that law which we once hated and which we had no ability to obey (Rom. 8:7-9). However, neither the work of Christ for us, nor the work of the Spirit in us, changes the righteous standard of the law or our obligation to keep it. God's grace gives us a heart to love what we once hated and an ability to keep, albeit imperfectly, yet evangelically and truly, that very law as a guide for our lives (Rom. 7:22; 8:3).

Recognizing the Ten Commandments as a summary of God's moral standard for His creatures, let us focus our attention upon the sixth commandment (Exod. 20:13). In it we are commanded, 'thou shalt not kill', or 'murder', as the original is sometimes rendered.

What does this commandment involve? Obviously it means that you should not take a pistol and put it to your neighbor's head and blow his brains out because he happened to run his car over your newly-seeded lawn. But, of course, it forbids far more than this. In the Westminster Larger Catechism there is some very helpful material regarding this, as well as for all the other commandments. Question 135 reads, 'What are the duties required in the sixth commandment?' The following are some selected segments from the answer given to that question. 'The duties required in the sixth commandment are *all careful studies, and lawful endeavors, to preserve the life of ourselves* and others by resisting all thoughts and purposes, subduing all passions, and *avoiding all occasions, temptations, and practices, which tend to the unjust taking away the life of any;...* a sober use of meat (food), drink, physic (medicine), sleep, labor, and recreations' (emphasis mine).

Question 136 reads, 'What are the sins forbidden in the sixth commandment?' Part of the answer given is: 'The sins forbidden in the sixth commandment are, ... *the neglecting or withdrawing the lawful and necessary means of preservation of life; ... immoderate use of meat (food), drink, labor, and recreations; ... and whatsoever else tends to the destruction of the life of any*'[1] (emphasis mine).

I would draw your attention particularly to several of the statements quoted above. Note that in answering the question concerning the *duties required* by this commandment, the framers of that catechism state that it is our duty to engage in 'all careful studies, and lawful endeavors, to preserve the life of ourselves and others.' In other words, they are asserting that the sixth commandment requires a conscientious effort to be reasonably knowledgeable concerning matters relative to our physical health and well-being. Furthermore, in identifying the *sins forbidden* by the sixth commandment they are asserting that it demands that we be conscientiously committed to 'avoiding all occasions, temptations, and practices, which tend to the unjust taking away the life of any.' If indeed we are under a moral obligation to engage in such studies and to avoid certain occasions, then we must not be willfully and perpetually ignorant or indifferent to the clearly established facts concerning

---

1   If the reader has never read the entire section in the Westminster Larger and Shorter Catechisms concerning the meaning of the Ten Commandments, the writer heartily recommends the exercise.

what comprises a healthy diet, and what constitutes adequate rest, or treat lightly the whole body of knowledge available to us in the book of general revelation concerning the means most calculated to contribute to the preservation of life.

General revelation does indeed yield revelatory data which God expects us to understand, believe and obey. Paul has no reservations in writing to the Corinthians, 'Does not nature itself teach you...?' (1 Cor. 11:14). It is an established fact of general revelation and nature that optimum physical health is most likely maintained with concern and effort to keep one's weight at a reasonable level, to engage in regular cardiovascular exercise and to make a habit of consuming nutritional foods and beverages rather than those that tend to undermine health.

Hence the first strand of the biblical antidote to preventing or curing that form of ministerial burnout resulting from attempting to live and labor as though you were a disembodied spirit is, by the power of the Holy Spirit and in virtue of your union with Christ, to seek to render evangelical obedience to the sixth commandment. To put it bluntly, we must not rob the Lord Jesus of an intended end of His suffering. This is precisely what we do if we are indifferent to our physical well-being. He died to make us evangelical law-keepers. One such law is that we shall do no murder. That commandment necessarily involves an understanding of and a practical commitment to the means calculated to the preservation of our own lives.

GLORIFY GOD IN YOUR BODY

The second strand of the antidote connected to this eighth warning is: *Remember your solemn obligation and privilege to glorify God in your body.*

Here the pivotal text is 1 Corinthians 6:19-20. The apostle is charging the Corinthians to avoid the sin of fornication. His focal point of concern is succinctly stated in verse eighteen, 'Flee from sexual immorality.' He sets that issue within a larger biblical principle or category of redemptive truth, which is characteristic of his pastoral manner. For example, when Paul gives specific instructions to husbands and wives concerning their roles and responsibilities within marriage, he sets forth profound truths concerning the relationship of Christ and His church (see Eph. 5:22-33).

Likewise, here in 1 Corinthians 6, while dealing primarily with sexual sin, the apostle gives us some of the richest teaching to be found anywhere in Scripture concerning how a Christian is to regard his body. For example, we are told in this passage that our bodies are nothing less than temples of the Holy Spirit. Furthermore, we are informed that we, including our bodies, have been purchased with a price. The command to glorify God in our bodies grows out of the fact that as Christians our bodies are the purchased possession of Jesus Christ and the very temple in which the Holy Spirit dwells. The God who purchased the temple has made it His own dwelling, in spite of all its weaknesses and its prospect of the grave until the resurrection. God informs us in the command to 'glorify God in your body' that we are to have a conscience bound by the duty of bringing praise and honor to Him in the theater of our bodies. The command is not that we glorify God *through* our bodies, but *in* them. Therefore, it can never be a valid spirituality which out of supposed love to Christ and professed obedience to the promptings of the Holy Spirit leads us to be abusive to our bodies, either by sins of omission or of commission.[2]

Scripture does demand that we deny bodily appetites that are inordinate and irregular. The apostle Paul said that he disciplined his body and kept it under, lest in preaching to others he should prove to be 'disqualified', the original word meaning 'not standing the test'[3] (1 Cor. 9:27). The apostle was

---

2   Many actual scholars consider the phrase, 'and in your spirit', to be of doubtful authorship. Perhaps they were added because the command to glorify God 'in your body' was considered to be less spiritual without the questionable phrase.

3   'ἀδόκιμος', BDAG lexicon. Arndt, W., Danker, F. W., & Bauer, W. (2000). A Greek-English lexicon of the New Testament and other early Christian literature (3rd ed.). Chicago: University of Chicago Press.

taking hold of his bodily appetites and restraining them with holy violence, lest through the corruption of his remaining sin they lead him into a course of sin. He uses a verb which could be literally rendered, 'to give a black eye'.[4] Very vivid imagery!

Furthermore, the Scriptures teach us that there are times when we should deny the body its legitimate and normal patterns of eating, drinking, sleeping and even sexual pleasures within the marriage bond, in order to engage in concentrated spiritual exercises. In addition to these qualifications, our Lord makes it clear in Matthew 10:28 that our primary concern must always be the salvation of our souls and not the preservation of our bodies. This qualification constitutes the fundamental justification for martyrdom. Notwithstanding, the imperative of 1 Corinthians 6:20 stands before all, mandating that you 'glorify God *in* your body'.

Several searching questions are now in order. May God enable each reader to ask these questions of himself with a present and felt consciousness that 'all are naked and exposed to the eyes of him to whom we must give account' (Heb. 4:13). Is God glorified in our bodies if we carelessly or knowingly rob them of the nutrients necessary by divine design in order for us to function at optimum efficiency and usefulness? Can we say that we are glorifying God in our bodies if we remain willfully ignorant of what those nutrients are and how best to secure their regular intake? Can we say that we are glorifying God in our bodies if we place them under undue stress because of the excessive use of caffeine, alcohol or an abundance of highly processed foods from which many of the God-implanted nutrients have been removed? Can we really say that we are glorifying God in our bodies if we knowingly clog up our arteries with undesirable plaque by a pattern of eating foods loaded with the kinds of fat which contribute to dangerously high cholesterol levels, thereby making ourselves candidates for

---

4   'ὑπωπιάζω', BDAG lexicon.

a serious heart attack or major heart surgery? Can we really say before God that we are glorifying Him in our bodies if by the accumulation of excessive and unhealthy weight we place an undue strain upon our knees, our hearts, and make ourselves highly vulnerable to diabetes and other debilitating diseases?[5] Can we say that we are glorifying God in our bodies, bodies He has made for action, if we abuse them by adopting a 'couch potato' (more likely for us as pastors, a 'desk potato') lifestyle rather than making ourselves engage in some regular forms of cardiovascular exercise?

In pressing these questions upon your conscience I am not implying that there may not be exceptional times of feasting when we can with a good conscience enjoy a modicum of the 'bad stuff'. When we are conscientiously seeking to glorify God in our bodies in our overall patterns of eating and exercise, we are then able with a good conscience occasionally to relax our normal disciplines of eating and exercise, only to take them up again after a brief suspension of them.

The right answer to these and many other similar questions is obvious. Therefore, my preacher brother, you must make it a matter of conscience before God that you will not only seek to render evangelical obedience to the broader commands and prohibitions of the sixth commandment, but that you will be committed in practical ways to obey the clear command to 'glorify God in your body'.

AN EXAMPLE TO THE FLOCK

There is a third strand in my proposed antidote to the burnout that comes from seeking to serve God as though we were disembodied spirits. In taking up this third strand I am moving

---

5   The World Health Organization wrote, 'Facts: Globally there are more than 1 billion overweight adults, at least 300 million of them obese. Obesity and overweight pose a major risk for chronic diseases, including type 2 diabetes, cardiovascular disease, hypertension and stroke, and certain forms of cancer. The key causes are increased consumption of energy-dense foods high in saturated fats and sugars, and reduced physical activity' (www.who.int/dietphysicalactivity/media/en/gsfs_obesity.pdf).

more onto the turf of 'ministerial washout' that is the erosion of our credibility as examples to our people. The third strand of exhortation is this: *Remember your solemn obligation to be an example to the flock of God in all things.*

This obligation is explicitly addressed in numerous passages. I will highlight only two of them. The first is found in Paul's words to Timothy, that young man who is in many ways the prototype of an evangelical minister. In 1 Timothy 4:12 the apostle says to his younger colleague, 'Let no one despise you for your youth, but set the believers an example in speech, in conduct, in love, in faith, in purity.' No minister who takes his Bible seriously would deny that he, like Timothy, is under a solemn obligation to be exemplary in speech, in love, in faith and in purity. But that is not all that the text addresses. Timothy must also be an example in his overall lifestyle. The word rendered 'conduct' is a word which speaks of one's general patterns of life. It could well be rendered 'way of life',[6] or in more contemporary jargon, one's 'overall lifestyle'.

What is one critical aspect of your overall lifestyle that is constantly on display before your people? Without doubt it is your physical appearance. Like it or not, you do not hover over the gathered congregation and interact with them as a disembodied spirit. They do not know that you are there present before them on the Lord's Day because your voice suddenly floats down upon them from above while they gaze upon an empty pulpit. They are not mesmerized by this heavenly voice, a voice speaking with such authority and celestial tones that they are utterly wrapped up in what you have to say with no thought whatsoever of how you look as you say it. I am conscious that this bit of fantasy borders on the ridiculous, but it does help to underscore the point. You appear before your people to lead them in worship and to preach to them in all the corporeal reality of your physical constitution. It is you in that body by which you are now

---

6   BDAG Lexicon, in loc.

holding and reading this book that they see. It is you in the totality of your humanity with whom they interact at the door as they leave the services on the Lord's Day. It is you, in the totality of your humanity, who is under a divine mandate to 'be an example to your people in all things', including the various disciplines that will be reflected in your physical condition. You are living before them as the embodiment of an example to be followed or rejected.

And consider these searching questions. Can you hold the consciences of your people in the iron grip of earned credibility when you seek to articulate the biblical teaching that radical discipleship – the only authentic kind – involves constant self-denial (Luke 9:23)? Can you expound the fact that the fruit of the Spirit is temperance or self-control (Gal. 5:22-23) and have the confidence that your physical appearance manifests that aspect of fruit produced by the Spirit? Like Solomon, can you warn your people of the dangers of the twin sins of drunkenness and gluttony and have your warnings stick because of the condition of your physical body as evidence of moderation and self-control in the use of food and drink? With respect to reasonably responsible patterns of diet and exercise, can you say to your people, 'Be imitators of me, as I am of Christ' (1 Cor. 11:1)?

The second text that must bind our conscience concerning our obligation to be an example to our people in all things is 1 Peter 5:3. Let us begin comment with verse one. Peter makes it evident that he is deliberately and specifically addressing the officially-recognized pastors of the churches in Asia Minor to whom his letter was sent. The central direction he gives these pastors is the imperative verb: 'Shepherd' the flock of God (v. 2). By apostolic mandate these men must fulfill the manifold duties of a shepherd to a flock of sheep. Peter then highlights in three negative/positive couplets issues relative to the motives and the manner in which they are to carry out this task of shepherding. 'Not for shameful gain, but eagerly; not domineering over those in your charge, but being examples to the flock' (vv. 2-3).

The capstone of all these directives is that these pastors must be examples to the flock. Peter is not saying that these pastors are to lead only or primarily by example any more than shepherds care for and lead their sheep primarily or exclusively by example. No, shepherds are to provide wise, loving, gracious, courageous, sacrificial and assertive leadership to their sheep (cf. Ps. 23; John 10:11-13). These spiritual shepherds are to give this kind of leadership while 'constantly inspecting and looking over the flock of God'.[7] Dropping the metaphorical language, Peter's insistence on exemplary pastors is this: Any time you call your people to any aspect of Gospel obedience, you must by God's grace seek to be, at least to some reasonable degree, the embodiment of the very thing to which you are calling them. This includes a willingness to confess sin and failure publicly when sin or failure has been publicly manifested. This is part of making yourself 'an example to the flock'. This is the very thing to which Paul was calling Titus when he wrote to him these words: 'show yourself in all respects to be a model of good works' (Titus 2:7).

Imagine with me that you lived in a little rural village where the dominant sin of the inhabitants was chronic alcohol abuse and drunkenness. Many of the citizens, most of the time, went about with red eyes, slurred speech, an unsteady gait and alcohol breath. In seeking to be a consistent Christian man shining as light in the midst of that crooked and twisted setting (Phil. 2:15), would you not consider it both your duty and your privilege to make it unmistakably evident that you were committed to a radically different lifestyle, a lifestyle which among other things would be radically different at the point of the dominant sin of the villagers? Your clear eyes,

---

7   Gk. ἐπισκοποῦντες, 'exercising oversight', may be spurious (see *A Textual Commentary on the Greek New Testament*, Bruce M. Metzger, in loc.). Nevertheless, the verb is a present active participle meaning 'to give attention to' and 'to accept responsibility for the care of someone' (BGAD Lexicon, in loc.).

articulate speech, steady walk and alcohol-free breath would be a constant and powerful witness to the transforming power of the Gospel.

Well, my brother, in our 'rural village' called the United States the statistical evidence is overwhelming that obesity with all of its attendant ills is a national epidemic among both the young and the old population. Anyone who doubts the validity of the statistics need only place himself in the middle of a local mall and observe the people as they pass by, or sit on a bench at an airport doing the same thing. In these two settings the statistics will be irrefutably validated right before your eyes.

Tragically, there is another setting in which the statistics are clearly validated. In recent years I have attended large gatherings of ministers where the degree of obesity among these evangelical and Reformed preachers was nothing short of shameful and scandalous. I am not referring to men who have allowed themselves to become a little pudgy. I am speaking of men who are grossly and obviously overweight. I know this is strong language. However, I have carefully weighed my words, and in the light of what I have seen with my own eyes my report is true. I am not indulging in rhetorical overkill.

Could it be that one of the reasons there has not been as extensive an outworking of the resurgence of Reformed truth into the ethical fabric of the many who have come to embrace that truth, is that many of the men who are preaching these truths are not themselves embodying the evident power of that truth in this very area of concern?

Let us return to my analogy of the village stigmatized by chronic alcohol abuse. Would we expect unconverted villagers to think that the Gospel was indeed a powerful, magnificent and glorious thing, if those of us who profess to believe it and claim to be transformed by it and even proclaim that Gospel of deliverance from drunkenness were going about with red eyes, unsteady gait, blurred speech and booze-tinged breath? By what specious and self-justifying logic can we escape the conclusion that our credibility as preachers, along with the credibility of the Gospel itself, is tragically eroded by bulging waistlines, jiggling jowls and puffy faces?

While writing these pages I have been rereading volume seven of John Owen's works. While identifying the causes of apostasy from the Gospel, he states one of the causes to be 'want (lack) of watchfulness against the insinuation of national vices and the prevailing sins of any present age.' He then elaborates:

> Hence the prevalency of the gospel in any nation may be measured by the success it hath against known national sins. If these are not in some good measure subdued by it, if the minds of men be not alienated from them and made watchful against them, if their guilt appear not naked, without the varnish or veil put upon it by commonness or custom, whatever profession is made of the gospel, it is vain and useless.[8]

With the ears of our hearts may we hear the searching and confirming words of Thomas Murphy as he underscores the crucial issue of the pastor's example:

> This appointment of the minister to teach by example must be carefully studied. All his other learning will be in vain without it. All other preparation for his office will be lost if this does not receive the chief attention. Of ministers emphatically it may be said that they are Christ's living epistles sent out into the world in order that men might read in them the transforming efficacy of his gospel.... Those who hold this office are not only to describe to men the effects of religion upon the life, but they are also to show them in their own practice.[9]

I would illustrate by an account I know for sure to be true. Once a pastor had a certain very athletic young man join the congregation. When he came into the church membership he

---

8   *The Works of John Owen*, VII, pp. 205-06.

9   Thomas Murphy, *Pastoral Theology*, (first published, 1877. Audubon, NJ: Old Paths Publications, 1996), pp. 57-58.

looked like he had just stepped out of a football player's locker room at one of the local colleges. He was six feet in height, and weighed approximately 240 pounds. It was 240 pounds of a well-conditioned athlete. In fact, he had actually played football as an interior lineman at one of the local colleges. After he joined the church, the pastor noticed that this young man was shedding a considerable amount of weight and inquired as to the reason why. His answer was along the following lines: 'Pastor, looking at you as a man in your mid-50s put me under conviction of sin. I now have no reason to weigh 240 pounds. I am not playing football any longer, and I am carrying around all that weight that does not glorify God. God convicted me by using your example. I have lost 30 pounds and I intend to keep it off.'

As of the writing of this book, that pastor is in his mid-70s, and he weighs the same or less than he did at the time this young man spoke to him. This fact is not the result of a natural and genetically programmed physical condition. Rather, it is the fruit of constant self-denial and discipline with respect both to food and to exercise. Each holiday season the few pounds that are added are consequently shed over the next several weeks by means of an intensified discipline. He has found that he who wins the battle with the three to five extra pounds will never have to enter a war with twenty-five to fifty extra pounds.

Some of my readers may think that I have spent an inordinate amount of time addressing this matter of our duty to be examples of the flock in this area of our physical appearance. However, I ask you to remember the words often attributed to Martin Luther. 'Where the battle rages, there the loyalty of the soldier is tested.' The battle rages at this point and I desire to be a loyal soldier.

TEN

Beware of Ministry with Neglect of Your Physical Body, Continued

I n this chapter we continue our consideration of the eighth warning against ministerial backsliding and burnout along with the additional issue that I have chosen to call 'credibility washout'. The warning is this: *Beware of seeking to serve God in the office and functions of the ministry as though you were a disembodied spirit, rather than a creature of flesh and blood.*

THE DIRECTIVES OF PAUL

I stated at the beginning of my treatment of this warning that I would consider five strands of the biblical antidote. I addressed the first three in the previous chapter. We now address the fourth and fifth strands, the fourth being: *Remember the specific directives of the apostle Paul which explicitly address the issue of Timothy's physical condition.*

In 1 Timothy 4:7 Paul charges Timothy, 'train yourself for godliness'. Then Paul makes a comparative statement of two positive assertions for motivating Timothy to fulfill this duty with diligence. The first assertion relates to 'bodily training', that it 'is of some value' (4:8), or, 'for a little is profitable' (word-for-word translation), with 'little' referring to the limited amount or limited time of the profit, benefit or usefulness (Gk. ὠφέλιμος) associated with bodily training. The second assertion is about the training which is for godliness, that it 'is of value in every way.' When the two forms of training are put into the arena to compete regarding their comparative worth, the training which is unto godliness will win the contest, hands down.

However, in setting forth the two forms of training and their comparative worth, the apostle does give us *two positive statements*. Bodily training is of some value, and training for godliness is also valuable. While Timothy must recognize the superior benefit of the training which is for godliness, Paul has said nothing to Timothy that would legitimately lead his younger colleague to despise or denigrate bodily training when kept in its proper place. Paul makes an explicitly positive statement when he writes that bodily training *is of some value*. He does not say that bodily training is useless, unnecessary, or that it should be regarded with indifference. It is of some value for the life that now is. Timothy would never have concluded from these words of Paul that he should put down the parchment on which they were written and think that he should be either ignorant or indifferent to the profit derived from bodily exercise.

If Timothy read the words of verse eight and concluded, 'Oh well, as I serve God in my ministerial calling I can forget bodily training of any kind because there is no value in it either in this world or in that which is to come,' he would have irresponsibly misconstrued the meaning of the apostle's words. No, Timothy would clearly understand from general revelation and from the words of Paul in this text that bodily training is of some value for the life which now is.

This is why the framers of the Westminster Larger Catechism say that the sins forbidden in the sixth commandment include 'the neglecting or withdrawing the lawful and necessary means of preservation of life' (Question 136). If bodily training is indeed profitable to the preservation of life, then indifference to such exercise is a willful robbing ourselves of that which God has created for our profit.

First Timothy 5:23 is a second text in the same sphere of concern. In its context, Paul is placing upon Timothy some very solemn and weighty ministerial responsibilities. While charging Timothy with performing these responsibilities, Paul wrote, 'No longer drink only water, but use a little wine for the sake of your stomach and your frequent ailments.' In the midst of charging Timothy with weighty ministerial responsibilities, why in the world does Paul suddenly assume the role of a non-licensed physician giving Timothy a prescription for a home remedy to deal with his chronic gastrointestinal disorders and other physical ailments? It seems to me that this is exactly what Paul is doing.

If this text teaches us anything, it is a reminder that Timothy does not carry out all those weighty and solemn ministerial tasks as a disembodied spirit. He has a gastrointestinal system which obviously undergoes chronic distress along with other chronic physical ailments. Paul is telling Timothy not to ignore the reality of those physical problems. Furthermore, he is telling Timothy that he wants him to take practical steps within the sphere of what is available to him for improving his physical condition that he might serve God with greater strength and vigor.

Now without a doubt Paul is suggesting to Timothy that the great tasks which have been laid upon him as a minister will ordinarily not be fulfilled by a man who is chronically sick, especially if his sickness remains for lack of due care and attention to a practical home remedy.

Calvin's comments on this verse are most perceptive:

> Now it is evident that Timothy was not only frugal, but even austere, in his mode of living; so much so as even not to take care of his health; and it is certain that this was done, neither through ambition nor through superstition. Hence we infer, that not only was he very far from indulging in luxury and superfluities, but that, in order that he might be better prepared for doing the work of the Lord, he retrenched a portion even of his ordinary food; for it was not by natural disposition, but through a desire of temperance, that he was abstemious.
>
> How few are there at the present day, who need to be forbidden the use of water; or rather how many are there that need to be limited to drink wine soberly! It is also evident how necessary it is for us, even when we are desirous to act right, to ask from the Lord the spirit of prudence, that he may teach us moderation. Timothy was, indeed, upright in his aims; but, because he is reproved by the Spirit of God, we learn that excess of severity of living was faulty in him. *At the same time a general rule is laid down, that, while we ought to be temperate in eating and drinking, every person should attend to his own health, not for the sake of prolonging life, but that, as long as he lives, he may serve God, and be of use to his neighbors* (author's emphasis).[1]

The last sentence in that quotation is profoundly important. It underscores the vital principle that our concern for physical health and well-being must not be that of feeding or promoting vanity, or primarily to pursue a long life for its own sake, but to have optimum usefulness in whatever years God entrusts to us.

My aim here is not to advocate moderate use of wine for gastrointestinal problems. Rather, I would convince you of the principle that in the midst of the most serious commitment to the full spectrum of our solemn ministerial duties it is not according to God's mind and will for us to neglect a conscientious effort for improving our native physical condition. That is the bottom line.

---

1 In loc.

A little wine will *not* be the remedy in most cases for our physical problems. Rather, it may be a little walk or a long walk. A little jogging or more than a little jogging. A little time on the treadmill or a little time on the weight machines at the local gym. A little this or a little that, but something that will clearly indicate our commitment to a responsible endeavor to bring ourselves to a greater level of physical health, vigor and strength, and to a physical condition and appearance that will be exemplary to our people.

A clear conscience and practical necessity require the use of appropriate means revealed in general revelation as Paul prescribed for Timothy.

While encouraging believers to be spiritually minded John Owen makes a very astute observation regarding the very issues we are addressing: 'If a man cannot obtain an athletic constitution of health, or a strength like that of Samson, yet, if he be wise, *he will not omit the use of such means* as may make him to be useful in the ordinary duties of life'[2] (author's emphasis).

LISTEN TO THE MASTERS
We come now to consider my fifth strand of counsel. Here, I will not attempt to bind the conscience of the reader, since what I will propose is derived from the sagacious advice and entreaties of men from the past rather than from the direct testimony of Scripture. *Soberly consider the wise counsel and the general consensus of proven guides concerning what is necessary to be an effective preacher.*

It is an interesting fact that one can read entire books on preaching and the work of the ministry written by our contemporaries and find little, if anything, that makes reference to the physical condition of the preacher. I am convinced that one of the reasons for this is that we suffer in our day from a lack of men who understand the rigors of true preaching. We have a host of Bible talkers who see no personal need to be in

---

2   *The Works of John Owen*, VII, p. 382.

sustained optimum physical condition to preach, even if they were to preach ten times a week. Such a schedule would not make any unusual demands upon their physical constitution.

However, the old masters understood that preaching was not just a mental exercise united to one's organs of speech. Rather, they understood that preaching worthy of its name engaged the whole of the preacher's redeemed humanity, and the entirety of that humanity brought to its most intense and vigorous exercise – mentally, emotionally and physically. Therefore, they understood physical conditioning in the life of the preacher to be a necessary and vital thing.

I now bring forward my first witness from the past. In his marvelously helpful book, *For the Work of the Ministry*, W. G. Blaikie, a nineteenth-century Scottish preacher and seminary professor, commented:

> It now remains to say a few words on *physical* preparation for preaching. The present generation is much more disposed than some of its predecessors to believe in a certain connection between good health and good preaching, although to many persons it may seem that there is no such connection, while a smaller number may think that a preacher's delicate health actually aids the right impression. And no doubt there is a certain class of truths which are taught more impressively by a man who bears the seal of death on his wasted face; but, on the other hand, such a man's influence in other respects is feeble, if not injurious. 'It is impossible,' says Mr. Beecher, 'for an invalid to sustain a cheerful and hopeful ministry among his people. An invalid looks with a sad eye on human life. He may be sympathetic, but it is almost always with the shadows that are in the world. He will give out moaning and drowsy hymns. He will make prayers that are almost all piteous. It may not be a minister's fault if he be afflicted and ill, and administers his duties in mourning and sadness, but it is a vast misfortune for his people.'

> The sad, somber, melancholy look of the invalid preacher, and, indeed, a heavy, dull, dreary look in any preacher, has

a specially repulsive effect on the young. It insensibly leads them to associate with church services the very opposite of those happy feelings which they so readily associate with their sports. Under any circumstances, the solemnity of divine worship constitutes something of a trial for the buoyant, playful tendencies of youth, but infinitely the more on that account is it a matter of regret if the trial is aggravated by the repulsiveness of a countenance on which nothing bright and radiant ever appears to settle.

But even where there is no positive disease, there may be a physical languor that reflects itself in feebleness of voice, dullness of tone, stiffness of manner, and a general want of lively and attractive power. It may be difficult to persuade some preachers that physical causes have to do with this, but the connection is beyond all reasonable doubt. And the fact that such symptoms are the effect *of some transgression of the laws of health* makes it incumbent upon the student to attend to the condition of his outer man (author's emphasis).[3]

Blaikie proceeds with some very specific counsel relative to the stomach, the nerves, the lungs,and the other organs of speech and the absolute necessity of recognizing what he calls 'the duty of caring for the health and vigor of the body'. As he draws to a conclusion this section of his lecture entitled 'Preparation for Preaching', he becomes quite pointed:

> *It is very certain that due attention to physical exercise is an essential condition of sustained vigorous preaching.* The command to be 'strong in the Lord' includes strength of body as well of strength of soul.

---

3   Regarding Blaikie, *The Dictionary of Scottish Church History and Theology* (IVP, 1993) says: 'Theologically he was in many respects conservative and was ill at ease with the liberalisation of the Free Church. Yet he enthusiastically advocated the new view of Scripture which sprang from biblical criticism and rejected the older theory of verbal inerrancy.' His contribution to the change in outlook in the nineteenth-century Free Church of Scotland Colleges regarding the inerrancy of the Bible is detailed in Kenneth R. Ross, *Church and Creed in Scotland*, (Rutherford House, Edinburgh, 1988) p. 188ff.

Some men may affect to despise these things, but it is a foolish affectation. Subordinate though their place may be, it is a real place notwithstanding; at least in every case where 'the bow abides in strength, and the arms of the hands are made strong by the hands of the mighty God of Jacob' (Gen. 49:24, author's emphasis).[4]

My second witness to the benefits of a pastor's commitment to regular physical exercise for improvement as a man and a preacher is Ebenezer Porter. He was the President and Professor of Sacred Rhetoric at Andover Seminary in the mid-1800s when that seminary was still committed to biblical truth. In his masterful and very detailed book entitled *Lectures on Homiletics* he deals very specifically with the preservation of one's vocal organs. In a passionate address to young men, he said:

While this object is in hand then, I affectionately offer you some admonitory remarks, in the hope that they may save some of you from those painful lessons, which so many have refused to learn from any teacher but experience. Nor am I such a novice in human affairs, as to expect that any counsels which I can give, by way of premonition, will be seasonably and seriously regarded by more than 1 in 10 of those to whom they are addressed. One who had the very best opportunities for observation on this subject, and was much distinguished too for discrimination of judgment, remarked to me, 'The student must break down *himself*, before he will take warning; very few men will learn anything, as to the preservation of health, from the experience of others.' Strange as it may seem, the great majority of students think precautions of this sort very proper for *others*, but altogether needless for *themselves*. So it has been, and so it probably will continue to be. Yet even in this unpromising aspect of the case, I will proceed; for should these admonitions be instrumental in saving a single young minister from the

---

4   William Garden Blaikie, *For the Work of the Ministry* (London: J. Nisbet, 1890) pp. 83-85.

premature sacrifice of himself, the labor of giving them will be a thousand-fold rewarded.[5]

Then after underscoring the fact that preachers are peculiarly vulnerable to certain physical liabilities because of their relatively sedentary lifestyle, he gives this practical advice:

> Do you ask how this train of calamities is to be avoided? The answer is, by a single prescription, the first, second, and third ingredient of which is – *exercise*. You ask *what* exercise? That depends on circumstances. Let some judicious physician, or other friend on whom you can rely, aid by his counsels, the suggestions of your own experience. With such assistance, and with the reserved privilege of often changing your choice, should the case require it, select that kind of exercise which is best suited to your own present condition. In general I will say, that exercise should be adapted to brace the muscular system, especially, the muscles of the chest and the gastric region; that it should be, as far as practicable, in the open air, and should be adapted to exhilarate the spirits.
>
> Whatever course is adopted, several things should be remembered – that more may be done in one day to confirm a sound constitution, than in one month to retrieve a broken one; that exercise, to be efficacious, must be regulated not by fits and impulses, but by a *vigorous system resolutely executed*; that its daily amount should be adjusted, not by an indolent temper, but by *religious principle,* according to the physical condition of the individual; and that this should be, in all cases, *not less than one hour*, before each meal, equivalent to labor; when the muscular power admits it, and when not, a longer time still, will be requisite for *passive* exercise.[6] (author's emphasis)

Porter then proceeds to make a somewhat humorous remark relative to the eating habits of the students to whom

---

5   Ebenezer Porter, *Lectures on Homiletics*, (no publisher listed, 1834), pp. 506-11

6   Passive exercise would refer to such things as horseback riding or riding in a horse-drawn carriage.

he ministered. With but little adjustment, they apply to preachers, whatever our age may be. Here are his remarks:

> I can hardly dismiss this topic without saying, that a judicious regard to *diet* is indispensable in guarding from disease of the vital organs of studious men. As I am not writing a medical treatise, it would be absurd for me to go into minute directions on this point. ... I will add the expression of my own decided belief, that while the amount of *exercise* taken by students (as well as preachers!) is generally too *little* by one half, the quantity of their food is too *great*, in about the same proportion.[7]

I now bring forward my third witness from the past, the inimitable C. H. Spurgeon. In his *Lectures to My Students*, he said:

> There can be little doubt that sedentary habits have a tendency to create despondency in some constitutions. Burton, in his *Anatomy of Melancholy*, has a chapter upon the cause of this sadness; and, quoting from one of the myriad authors whom he lays under contribution, he says:
>
> > 'Students [preachers of any age as well – author's comment] are negligent of their bodies. Other men look to their tools; a painter will wash his pencils; a smith will look to his hammer, anvil, forge; a husbandman will mend his plough-irons, and grind his hatchet if it be dull; a falconer or huntsman will have an especial care of his hawks, hounds, horses, dogs, etc.; a musician will string and unstring his lute; only scholars neglect that instrument (their brains and spirits I mean) which they daily use. Well saith Lucan, 'See thou twist not the rope so hard that it break.'
>
> To sit long in one posture, poring over a book, or driving a quill [holding a pen or tapping a computer keyboard – author's comment], is in itself a taxing of nature; but add to

---

7   Porter, *Lectures on Homiletics*, pp. 506-11

this a badly-ventilated chamber, a body which has long been without muscular exercise, and a heart burdened with many cares, and we have all the elements of preparing a seething cauldron of despair, especially in the dim months of fog....

A day's breathing of fresh air upon the hills, or a few hours' ramble in the beech woods' umbrageous calm, would sweep the cobwebs out of the brain of scores of our toiling ministers who are now but half alive. A mouth full of sea air, or a stiff walk in the wind's face, would not give grace to the soul, but it would yield oxygen to the body, which is the next best.[8]

One of the many things I love about Spurgeon is that he recognized that grace does not war with nature. He proved his solid grasp upon this truth when he wrote, 'The next best thing to the grace of God for a preacher is oxygen.'[9]

With measured approval Spurgeon quotes an American preacher who said that 'the best preparation for preaching is to get a good night's rest, and to eat a good breakfast.'[10] He gives the following practical and very earthy advice in his famous lectures to 'gentlemen with narrow chests': 'use the dumb-bells every morning, or, better still, those clubs which the College has provided for you.'[11] Spurgeon's advice was to 'pump iron', so to speak.

While I trust that each of my readers embraces in some crucial areas a better theology than his, John Wesley has some very helpful advice to give us regarding physical exercise. He wrote, 'Today I entered on my eighty-second year, and found myself just as strong to labor, and as fit for any exercise of body or mind, as I was forty years ago.'[12] To what did he attribute this? In his entry to his journal on June 28, 1778, at age 85 he

---

8   C.H. Spurgeon, *Lectures to my students* (first published, 1875-94. Edinburgh: Banner of Truth, 2008), pp. 183-84.

9   Ibid., p. 148.

10   *An All Round Ministry*, p. 136.

11   *Lectures*, p. 141.

12   *Journal*, Number 20, p. 296.

said it was due first to God's power and to the prayers of God's children, but also to his 'constant exercise and change of air.'[13] To his perspectives we could add those of a host of others.

Brethren, we are not wise if we do not listen to the counsel of these sagacious men who lived long enough to observe and to articulate with astute perception the fact that as an ordinary rule, the preacher who neglects sufficient physical culture will eventually pay dearly for that neglect.

Also, I plead with you seriously to consider the counsel of the masters of medicine and nutrition. God has permitted us to live at a time when from general revelation a number of indisputable axioms relative to physical health and well-being have been identified and articulated. For example, I trust that I need not attempt to convince you that there is now no question concerning the direct connection between cigarette smoking and lung cancer. You will not find this fact asserted in your Bible but in the book of general revelation. There is also an equally well-established medical consensus concerning the direct connection between the absence of regular and sustained cardiovascular exercise and incidents of premature cardiac degeneracy, excessive weight gain and a host of other physical maladies.

We believe that this is God's world and that God speaks in general revelation. When we rightly understand His voice speaking in general revelation it will never contradict the precepts or principles of special revelation. It is a bogus spirituality that would lead any man to stop his ears to the voice of general revelation as it is heard in the well-established medical facts concerning the health-yielding benefits of proper diet, reasonable weight control and regular exercise.

In the light of these things I should like to offer some very practical advice.[14] First of all, if you have not recently undergone

---

13   Cited in *The Works of Wesley*, Vol. 5, 'The Life of the Rev. John Wesley,' p. 52.

14   This advice applies to those who have various medical services available to them. For any who may be reading these pages who do not have these services, you must seek out whatever appropriate means are available to you in your present circumstances.

a complete physical examination, including extensive blood analysis and an EKG, I would urge you to do so as soon as possible. If the blood work reveals abnormally high cholesterol levels, commit yourself to those changes in your diet, weight control and exercise which will usually appreciably improve cholesterol levels. Do not immediately run to the use of the various medications prescribed for high cholesterol. All of them have some measure of negative side effects. If a change of diet and patterns of exercise do not resolve the problem, then perhaps you ought to consider the moderate use of one of the medications calculated to address this problem. Also, if your EKG shows any abnormality, you ought to seek the input of a responsible cardiologist, who will most likely recommend a stress test and pictures of your heart.

In addition I would urge you to find a doctor who will be honest with you about your present weight and whether or not you ought to establish a lower target weight. Then, if it is decided that you ought to lose considerable weight, obtain some responsible material on nutritional matters. Beware of crash diets and weight loss programs that advocate a radical imbalance of the kinds of food that are recommended. At the end of the day there is a simple and iron-clad formula that is operative for all of us when it comes to the matter of our weight. The formula is this: what goes in, minus what goes out, minus what is burned up, stays on. If too much is staying on, then it is clear that less must go in or more must be burned up. For the person who is grossly overweight, both the amount that is taken in and the activities that will result in burning up what is taken in must be radically altered, resulting in a lifetime change of lifestyle.

Furthermore, if it is clear that you must lose considerable weight it is generally very helpful to establish a pattern of a weekly 'weigh in' and to make yourself accountable to a trusted brother in the Lord to whom you will report what the scales tell you. While we readily play head games with ourselves when it comes to the matter of weight control, a trustworthy scale will never lie to us or flatter us. Its numbers look up at our eyes and always tell us the truth. Scales have a strict conscience concerning the ninth commandment!

If you have not been engaged in some form of regular cardiovascular exercise, and if your general physical exam does not reveal some reason why you should not engage in such exercise, you must determine before God that this will now become an integral part of your life. Be sure to start with a modest program of such exercise. Many years ago, for me, this meant jogging around my backyard until I could begin to run on the sidewalk in my neighborhood, starting with just 6/10 of a mile. Beginning with a modest endeavor is crucial. Few things are more discouraging when seeking to establish a new discipline than failure to attain the standards of an overly ambitious beginning.

Then, once committed to such an exercise program, be determined that you will stick to that program regardless of what you feel like. Remember the words of Ebenezer Porter that we need to be committed to a 'vigorous system resolutely executed'. In the same way that you stick to your scheduled times of Bible reading, prayer and sermon preparation, regardless of how you may feel when you come to the time allocated for those activities, you must conscientiously stick to your exercise program. If I were to exercise only when I have felt like it I do not know what kind of shape I would be in today. Almost every time I come to my scheduled exercise time I am conscious that there is an aversion to that activity, an aversion rooted in my remaining sin. It is when we would do good that we are most conscious that the evil of remaining sin is with us (Rom. 7:21). There is a tape recording in my brain containing every imaginable reason to skip my planned exercise regimen. That tape is activated almost every time I purpose to put on my exercise outfit and make my way to the gym. I have never been one who experiences an 'exercise high.' The only 'high' I receive is that of a good conscience when I have by the grace of God done what I know I should have done in terms of keeping my appointed exercise regimen.

We have been privileged to witness things in our generation that would make some of our spiritual forefathers dance with joy. In many places there has been an evident return to the old paths. There has been a renewed commitment to the centrality of preaching. There has been a new appreciation of the benefits and blessings of vigorous, animated, urgent and passionate biblical preaching. However, we will not be able to engage in such preaching over the long haul if we are indifferent to our physical condition.

Hence with deep urgency I have laid before you this eighth word of counsel with respect to the avoidance of ministerial backsliding, burnout and credibility washout. It does not matter that we have learned from Christian biography that there were certain preachers who were greatly blessed of God while they obviously neglected the proper care of their bodies. We leave them, their ministries and their delinquency in this matter with God. However, our lives should be framed by the precepts and principles of the Word of God. I trust sufficient biblical evidence has been brought forward to persuade your conscience that this eighth warning is indeed a valid one: *beware of seeking to serve God in the office and functions of the ministry as though you were a disembodied spirit, rather than a man of flesh and blood.* In response to these things, remember that 'whoever knows the right thing to do and fails to do it, for him it is sin' (James 4:17).

Restoration

Of The

Convicted Pastor

ELEVEN

Five Closing Counsels to Remember

The eight warnings against ministerial backsliding and burnout have been articulated, along with a warning concerning 'credibility washout'. The symptoms, causes and cures for these conditions have been addressed.

I stated in the introduction to this book that I wrote it seeking to envision a group of godly pastors sitting before me, eager to discover and deal with any manifestations of ministerial backsliding and burnout. I am now imagining that after delivering the burden of these pages, I have that same group of pastors before me ready to engage in a question and answer session.

I am quite certain that one of the first questions that would be raised would be along these lines: 'Brother Martin, the Lord has used what you have conveyed to us to show me some specific areas of sin, of culpable ignorance, and of carnal indifference concerning ministerial backsliding and burnout. Where do I go from here?' This final chapter is calculated to give some concrete biblical counsel in answer to that question.

As each of the warnings began with the word 'beware', each of these words of counsel will begin with the word 'remember.' And the first is this: *Remember that if God has used these pages to wound you, it has been in order to show Himself to you as a gracious God who delights to heal you.*

God says, 'See now that I, even I, am he, and there is no god beside me; I kill and I make alive; I wound and I heal' (Deut. 32:39). Again, God gives a gracious invitation and promise to His backslidden people Israel, 'Return, O faithless sons; I will heal your faithlessness' (Jer. 3:22). Then recall the prophet Hosea's tender word, 'Come, let us return to the Lord; for he has torn us, that he may heal us; he has struck us down, and he will bind us up' (Hosea 6:1).

When we grasp the principle that God does not wound us only to leave us groveling and wallowing in the blood of His love wounds, we will then find ourselves praying in the language of the prophet Jeremiah, 'Heal me, O Lord, and I shall be healed; save me, and I shall be saved, for you are my praise' (Jer. 17:14). It is a cause of deep grief to God when, in tender love, He wounds His children in order to bring them to true repentance to the end that their fellowship with Him might be restored and deepened, and they allow the wound to drive them away from the God who has inflicted it. My dear brother, He who has exposed your backsliding, who has tenderly shown you the causes of your burnout, and has smitten you sharply for your credibility washout, is the gracious Savior, even the God who has promised that 'a bruised reed he will not break, and a faintly burning wick he will not quench' (Isa. 42:3).

My second word of counsel is: *Remember the necessity of dealing with your backsliding, burnout and washout in a thoroughly gospel or evangelical way.*

My dear fellow servant of God, remember that your backslidings, whatever has been their cause, and your burnout, whatever its contributing factors may have been, and even your credibility washout, whatever specific inconsistencies have produced it – none of these things have altered your standing before God in Christ. You are still a man who has 'been justified by faith' in Christ (Rom. 5:1). You are still an adopted son of God, fully and freely 'blessed . . . in the Beloved' One (Eph. 1:6). Your perseverance in the way of truth and holiness is yet being secured by the intercession of your great High Priest (Heb. 7:25; John 17:17) and by the ministry of the indwelling Holy Spirit, by whom you have been 'sealed for the day of redemption' (Eph. 4:30).

All of my subsequent counsel is given assuming that by renewed exercises of faith you will experience a fresh sense of these gospel realities and that you will be determined to deal with your backsliding, burnout and washout in such a way as to make these precious truths of gospel experience even more precious. I have absolutely no interest whatsoever in promoting any kind of mere behavior modification. Remember our Lord's description of what happens when an unclean spirit has gone out of a man, but then returns to its former house and, finding it empty, brings with it seven other spirits more wicked than itself (Matt. 12:43-45). My concern is to give counsel that with the blessing of the Holy Spirit will result in nothing less than evangelical repentance leading to evangelical reformation and transformation. By this I mean repentance and reformation drenched with gospel motives and empowered by gospel dynamics – Christ and His cross, Christ and His intercession, Christ by His indwelling Spirit, Christ and His promised enablement, the Father and His principled and wise pruning of fruitful branches, the Father and His willingness to give the Spirit to His children, the Father and His tender concern for us in our weakness – these are the things that constitute the wonderful raw materials of gospel motives and gospel dynamics.

In other words the counsel which remains assumes that you know and believe that the entire Godhead – Father, Son, and Holy Spirit – is committed to restore your backsliding, to heal your burnout and to recover the ground lost by your washout. Believing this will enable you to consider the remaining counsel with gospel hope and expectation for healing and recovery.

And so my third word of counsel is this: *Remember the unalterable necessity of dealing by deep and thorough gospel repentance with the sins leading to and attending your backsliding, burnout and washout.*

In taking up this concern perhaps no text in all of the Word of God is more relevant than Proverbs 28:13 which reads as follows: 'Whoever conceals his transgressions will not prosper, but he who confesses and forsakes them will obtain mercy.' If you would know spiritual prosperity once more then there must be an exercise of judgment-day honesty in dealing with the sins which have led to your backsliding, burnout and washout, and also with the sins that have been the fruit of these conditions. If you try to conceal those sins God himself will lock you up in a prison house of non-prosperity. You *will not* prosper.

Examples of this 'deep and thorough gospel repentance' are found in such passages as Psalm 51, in the disposition and language of the returning prodigal in Luke 15 and in 2 Corinthians 7:10-11, one of the most comprehensive descriptions of this kind of repentance.

The nature of the sins repented of and brought to the 'fountain opened ... to cleanse ... from sin and uncleanness' (Zech. 13:1) may be such as to demand confession and the seeking of forgiveness at the horizontal level as well. There probably are more than a few people against whom you have sinned in your state of backsliding, burnout and washout. Among them will be, most likely, your wife, your children and the flock of God in which God has placed you as an overseer. You must be willing to own your sins and to seek forgiveness from those who have been affected. Here I am not referring to the insipid pattern of 'apologizing', popular in our day. I am speaking about true repentance. This involves specifically naming and acknowledging one's sin as sin, and humbly seeking forgiveness from the offended party or parties.[1]

We do well to remember that the Bible does clearly indicate that there are circumstances in which we are to 'confess your sins to one another' (James 5:16). Further, since the Scriptures command, 'Be kind to one another, tenderhearted, forgiving one another, as God in Christ forgave you' (Eph. 4:32), is there not a clear assumption that we will be seeking forgiveness one of another as part of normal Christian experience? Again, remember that the Lord Jesus says, 'Pay attention to yourselves! If your brother sins, rebuke him, and if he repents, forgive him, and if he sins against you seven times in the day, and turns to you seven times, saying, "I repent", you must forgive him' (Luke 17:3-4). Here again we face the assumption that our sins at the horizontal level will necessitate repentance and confession at that level.

Some readers may judge this prescription for dealing thoroughly with the sins connected with our backsliding, burnout and credibility washout as being overly demanding. However, without such thorough dealing with our sin the indictment given through the prophet Jeremiah will have a crippling contemporary application. Jeremiah 6:14 indicts false prophets this way: 'They have healed the wound of my people lightly, saying, "Peace, peace", when there is no peace.'

James wrote, 'Draw near to God, and he will draw near to you. Cleanse your hands, you sinners, and purify your hearts, you double-minded. Be wretched and mourn and weep. Let your laughter be turned to mourning and your joy to gloom. Humble yourselves before the Lord, and he will exalt you' (James 4.8-10). If ever these words should be laid to heart and shape our spiritual responses, it is upon the discovery of

---

1 Chapter four illustrates with the confession of a lie uttered in the act of preaching.

a serious case of ministerial backsliding or ministerial credibility washout.

However, this repentance must be *gospel* repentance. Such repentance has one eye fixed on the heinousness of our sin, but the other eye must be steadily and believingly fixed on the only divine remedy for sin, even our crucified and now exalted Savior. We must resort again and again to 1 John 1:9–2:1 as our only refuge.

In this process of recovery from ministerial backsliding and burnout, and also from credibility washout, we must, in the fourth place, *Remember God's gracious provisions which have furnished us with the power to change the patterns and practices which have produced our backsliding, burnout and washout.*

God is not like the harsh and unreasonable taskmasters of Egypt who demanded bricks without providing straw. Rather, God has 'granted to us all things that pertain to life and godliness' (2 Pet. 1:3).

We must know and believingly appropriate the significance of the following gracious provisions of God given to enable us to make real changes:

1. The facts and implications of our union with Christ (Rom. 6:1-14; John 15:1-8; Col. 2:6-7; Gal. 2:20; Col. 3:1-3).

2. The fact and implications of the personal indwelling of the Holy Spirit (Rom. 8:7-9, 13; Gal. 5:22-3; Phil. 2:12-13; Luke 11:13; 2 Cor. 3:18).

3. The exceeding great and precious promises of the Word of God (2 Pet. 1:2-4; John 15:7).

4. The privilege of free access to the throne of grace and to a loving heavenly Father's provisions (Heb. 4:16; Matt. 7:7-11).

5. The fellowship, life and various ministries of the church of Christ (Eph. 4:1-16; Acts 2:42; Heb. 10:24-25).

These five things do not constitute an exhaustive list of the gracious provisions of God by which we are enabled to make real changes. However, they do represent His central provisions so we can come from a backslidden to a spiritually healthy state, from burnout to a vigorous and resilient state, and from washout to a state of earned credibility before our people.

My final word of counsel is this: *Remember that immediate, diligent, Christ-dependent efforts to implement the necessary changes to recover from ministerial backsliding, burnout and washout is the only proof of your having had and continuing to experience authentic dealings with God.*

We are all masters of self-deception. James understood this well when he wrote, 'But be doers of the word, and not hearers only, deceiving yourselves' (James 1:22). The deception to which James refers occurs when we think we are better men simply because we have heard and received the Word, perhaps even with a measure of delight and other appropriate emotional responses, like the rocky ground hearers in the parable of the sower, who received the word with joy (Matt. 13.20). However, unless what we have heard actually regulates our conduct, our hearing with delight and consent only leaves us in the delusion that we are better men for our hearing.

My preacher brother, if you are to profit from the counsels given in this book then you must be able to say with the psalmist, 'When I think on my ways, I turn my feet to your testimonies; I hasten and do not delay to keep your commandments' (Ps. 119:59-60).

I conclude this book with that wonderful prayer and benediction (Heb. 13:20-21) given to us by the Holy Spirit: 'Now may the God of peace who brought again from the dead our Lord Jesus, the great shepherd of the sheep, by the blood of the eternal covenant, equip you with everything good that you may do his will, working in us that which is pleasing in his sight, through Jesus Christ, to whom be glory forever and ever. Amen.'

Christian Focus Publications

Our mission statement –

STAYING FAITHFUL

In dependence upon God we seek to impact the world through literature faithful to His infallible Word, the Bible. Our aim is to ensure that the Lord Jesus Christ is presented as the only hope to obtain forgiveness of sin, live a useful life and look forward to heaven with Him.

Our Books are published in four imprints:

CHRISTIAN
FOCUS

Popular works including biographies, commentaries, basic doctrine and Christian living.

CHRISTIAN
HERITAGE

Books representing some of the best material from the rich heritage of the church.

MENTOR

Books written at a level suitable for Bible College and seminary students, pastors, and other serious readers. The imprint includes commentaries, doctrinal studies, examination of current issues and church history.

CF4•K

Children's books for quality Bible teaching and for all age groups: Sunday school curriculum, puzzle and activity books; personal and family devotional titles, biographies and inspirational stories – Because you are never too young to know Jesus!

Christian Focus Publications Ltd,
Geanies House, Fearn, Ross-shire,
IV20 1TW, Scotland, United Kingdom.
www.christianfocus.com